LOST
on the **PGA** *and*
EUROPEAN TOURS

LOST

on the **PGA** *and* EUROPEAN TOURS

A Memoir by JOCELYN HEFNER

Archway Publishing books may be ordered through booksellers or by contacting:

Archway Publishing
1663 Liberty Drive
Bloomington, IN 47403
www.archwaypublishing.com
1 (888) 242-5904

Because of the dynamic nature of the Internet, any web addresses or links contained in this book may have changed since publication and may no longer be valid. The views expressed in this work are solely those of the author and do not necessarily reflect the views of the publisher, and the publisher hereby disclaims any responsibility for them.

Any people depicted in stock imagery provided by Thinkstock are models, and such images are being used for illustrative purposes only. Certain stock imagery © Thinkstock.

"She Let Go" used with permission from Reverend Safire Rose.

ISBN: 978-1-4808-2423-2 (sc)
ISBN: 978-1-4808-2425-6 (hc)
ISBN: 978-1-4808-2424-9 (e)

Library of Congress Control Number: 2015918945

Print information available on the last page.

Archway Publishing rev. date: 12/10/2015

For ten years I shared my life with Paul Casey. While we lived, loved and celebrated many aspects of life on the PGA and European Tours we also learned a lot about life. My journey with him will forever be in my heart.

Dedication

This story is dedicated to the men and women who have sacrificed their own dreams for the love of another person. If you are standing in a bookstore or have this book in your hand, know it is divinely guided. It is my sincere desire that the messages shared here will embrace your heart and invite you to live fully from the center of your being.

Contents

Part III: Finding Purpose *169*

Appendix of Blog Entries *215*

Introduction

I HAVE CHOSEN NOT TO USE PAUL'S NAME IN THIS BOOK AND am instead using "him." I am doing this because my story is a universal one and "him" could be the person in anyone's life.

Perhaps you have heard the rumor that there is a story inside each of us that longs to be told. I love this rumor. I love to read true stories about how someone was headed in one direction, and then suddenly everything changed. These are the stories that help me to know I am not alone and, despite how it feels at times, I am not crazy.

One day, a quiet whispering in my heart let me know it was time for my story to be told. I never dreamed that I would be sharing what you are about to read, because I have always been one to keep my deepest feelings in a vault. I didn't want you to know much about me. I was afraid you might discover that, on the inside, I was not who I appeared to be on the outside.

I played catch-me-if-you-can with everyone—that is, until the game reversed.

You see, I was one of those young girls born into an affluent family who always wanted more than what was in front of her. I was restless, never satisfied, on a mission, and didn't want anyone to help me. I wanted to be the best at everything: the first one to answer a question, the last one to ever give up. I loved to be alone in my room, dreaming about how one day I would be a respected international interior designer. I would be the best, the best in the whole world. I would have the best horses and travel the world, competing in the best equestrian competitions. I would have and be the best of everything.

All my plans were set. I was one of fifteen people to be accepted into the Design School of London. I had earned countless blue ribbons in equestrian sports all over the United States and in Canada. I was on my way—until my journey was derailed when I made the choice to follow his dream rather than my own.

This story is about what happened: the personal account of my self-discovery while traveling for ten years on the PGA and European tours with a professional golfer. While I was traveling to some of the most renowned golf courses in the world, the shadows deep within my heart were finally exposed.

All alone in my sometimes opulent hotel rooms, as he practiced before the tournament, I gradually became emotionally disconnected from my own voice and my own truths. I began to pay attention only to *his* world. I became caught up in the glamour of the professional golf tours. That is, until he told me our marriage was over.

In order to live, I had to crawl out of the fog of denial to face the enormity of the impact of my perfectionism and my fearful feeling that I was never enough. Finally, I wasn't the best. I couldn't fix it, and I did not know how to return to my own journey. I had given it all up for him: my dreams, my voice, my whole heart. The crazy thing is that he never asked me to. He was the one who wanted me to have my own career. He was the one who relentlessly supported my dreams. It was me, so desperate to marry one of the best, who lost myself.

This is not a victim's story. Nor is it a story to glorify him. We all know we have so many character flaws that if a video camera were filming our inner and outer lives, most of us would be mortified to see our behavior, let alone our judgmental thoughts. Simply, we all have our "stuff." This story is about *my* stuff and how, in the heat of the pain, I was thrust into roaring hot fires so the layers of distortions could take me further and further into the shadows of my small self, only for me to return to my real self.

As you read my account, I want you to try to remember that today, I see living and traveling with him only as the backdrop for my journey to finding me again. I have no desire in any way to disrespect him or the tours. My years with him will forever remain etched in my heart as the setting to expose my inner light and inner shadows. Without the lessons I learned being with him, I would not be living the life of inner freedom that I desire to live today. I am so grateful for all of it.

In this book, I invite you to explore the inner terrain of your own lives, asking what price you pay in your heart if you are living a life in fear of abandonment, of not being enough—if you are bypassing your feelings. What risks of the heart are truly worth taking? I am also sharing the journey of finding my way back through the pain, the heartache, and the beliefs that no longer served me.

Today, I hold hands with all the men and women who progressively dim their own passions in order to be loved, to fit in, and to live the American Dream. This book is one of my contributions to the importance of sharing our personal stories of returning to who we really are. I hope you find something in my story that helps you. That's all I want.

This is my story, not his story.

In the course of describing my journey up to now, it has been very challenging to write about the person I am not today. The person who is sharing her story today retains the memories of her journey, but no longer identifies with her lost self. I am also aware that I am sharing my story before I have entered the second half of my life. I continue to have much to learn on this incredible journey of awakening awareness about who I am and my place in the world.

The inner door to my return to my essential truths and nature did not happen through a car accident, a medical diagnosis, or a loss of income. My suffering was in a decadent setting while living the "American Dream." For those who have awakened to their separation from who they are in more downtrodden, poverty-stricken places, I hope you can make room for the pain that can exist at all economic levels and know that the yearning for inner peace and meaning is universal.

I have read many personal journeys, mostly by people who have traveled their paths many more years than I have. This is one of the reasons I am sharing my story. Often, as I was seeking truth, I longed to read stories of people like me, who had not traveled to India to study with a guru, sat in ashrams for years in silence, or studied all of the world's religions and wisdom. I longed for teachers and books that offered direct guidance in language I could understand. As you will see, I was led to a place and to experiences that respected the return to our true natures without having to live an isolated life or use fancy terms.

More and more, I meet others who are awakening to their inherent spiritual natures; some are in my age group and some are younger. At the time of this writing, I am in my mid thirties.

Many of us are seeking our spiritual return outside of religion. I am also aware that people in the evening of their lives are seeking new spiritual understanding of themselves. No matter what stage of life, the call to the gift we are on earth to give is real; it is true. The journey to finding this gift often requires suffering—crucifixion.

The journey to expressing our unique gifts requires conviction, courage, and connecting with others who have gone before us—resurrection.

In my story, you will see that I was given an unexpected gift: a glimpse into perspectives about myself and life that I didn't know existed. The shattering of my personal identity was terrifying. Returning to my real self was extraordinary. I will whisper forever and ever—*thank you to all the people who helped me.*

Part I:
The Early Years

The Beginning

EVERY STORY HAS A BEGINNING. OUR STORY STARTED WHEN I was twenty-one and he was twenty-four. I was standing in front of the Heron Bay Hotel on March 7, 2001, in Coral Springs, Florida. He walked up to me and told me he liked the Union Jack flag printed on my T-shirt. I was glad I had worn it with my knee-length white jeans and favorite black sandals. I would have never dreamed this would be the conversation starter with the man I would eventually marry.

I attended this particular tournament because my sister Jenny had married Fulton Allem, a tour player from South Africa. She asked if I would travel with them to take care of my precious niece, Sybil, so she could watch Fulton play. I said yes because I wanted to help her out; otherwise, I would not have gone to this tournament.

I couldn't tell you what attracted me to him the most: his Issey Miyake cologne, his English accent, his square-toed shoes, or his big smile. I was casually talking with Fuzzy Zoeller when he walked into the lobby bar. Fuzzy, being a real character—and one of three golfers to have won the Masters Tournament in his first Masters event—formally introduced us before walking out the door and leaving us alone to get to know each other.

Our initial conversation wasn't like most meetings for me with a handsome man. He seemed interested in getting to know me rather than talking about himself. You would have thought I hadn't talked about myself in years when on that first night I ended up telling him my whole life story. At least, I told him the parts of my story that I wanted him to know. I couldn't believe he was asking so many questions about my life.

Knowing he played on both the US and European tours was hugely attractive. However, the real hook that made me want to sit with him until the wee hours of the morning was his continual "tell me more" attitude. At one point he leaned into me while looking into my eyes, and I thought I was going to faint. I was completely disarmed by his intense sincerity. I loved that he was so engaging. I wasn't used to it. I felt like I was somebody when I was sitting with him. I was somebody. He was somebody. We could be somebody, and he took residence in my heart that night in the hotel lobby. Later in my room, as I drifted into sleep, I wondered if I had checked in to his heart.

I kept reviewing what I had said to him. *Did I tell him too much? Did I look okay? Could he feel how self-conscious I was?* He seemed so confident. When he said he needed to get to bed because of his morning tee time, I wondered if that was true or if he was bored with me. I wished he had kissed me. Just a little kiss, that's all; but he didn't.

I couldn't quite grasp why he seemed to want to know so much about me. With other men, I was the question asker, not the talker. I always allowed them to ramble on and on, talking mostly about how great they were. I honestly did not know how to stop them. I wouldn't go out with them again. From the time I was a child, I had found it difficult to engage in a back-and-forth conversation. I was a better listener than I wanted to be and lived on the periphery of conversations.

I was a fairly serious little girl, always trying to accomplish something. At eight years old, I created a plan to buy my own horse. I saved all my money from working in my dad's produce business, out in the fields under the Florida sun. I carried a yellow legal pad to write down all the information I needed in order to sell my parents on the idea. Like my dad, I relentlessly kept my eye on the goal and learned about endurance and commitment. Everyone told me I was a perfectionist. They were right.

It has taken many years for me to get that perfectionism is also a characteristic of professional athletes. I've seen and heard that many people at the top of their game consider perfectionism the price of admission to be in the big leagues. No wonder he was initially attracted to my attention to detail, my desire to be in control of my environment, and my drive to have the best in every aspect of my life. What neither of us understood was that my game was different. My perfectionism had permeated my entire life, creating rigid oppression everywhere I looked. In my healing process, I began to see that my perfectionist mind had advanced to the stage where any tiny human mistake registered in my brain as a total failure.

I didn't know my entire identity was dependent upon his succeeding and winning. There were moments when he didn't do as well in a golf tournament as he wanted to, and I thought it was *my* fault. I didn't know my increasing rigidity was caused by my intense self-scrutiny, self-criticism, and self-doubt. I observed many pro golfers display their disappointment when they missed the shot they so desperately wanted to make; however, I watched them learn from their mistakes and live in the solution and not the problem. I didn't have that skill ... yet.

I also heard many of the players talking about performance anxiety. It was no secret that the enormous pressure they were under wasn't easy. They hired sports psychologists, took mind discipline and mindfulness training, and didn't seem ashamed of their natural, human characteristics. I was different. Until I couldn't control the outcome of my marriage, I would never, ever have admitted I was anxious or afraid of anything. I played everything safe. I calculated risks carefully for fear of exposing a mistake. Simply, perfectionism had been running me, but to him, it looked good. I wasn't just a pretty girl. I appeared to have substance and was always on task. I didn't chatter on and on mindlessly about this and that. He had no idea that my inner chatter was calculating when to be silent and when to talk and what, exactly, to say.

In my healing journey, I learned what programmed my desire to be perfect. I began to see how my fear of failure both served and hurt me. I learned about the aspect of me that always desires more and is never satisfied. I witnessed this part of me running around, creating a knot of tension and suffering within and without. I became acquainted with the part of me that was constantly striving to meet everyone's expectations.

The good news was that eventually I learned my perfectionism was only a part of me. While this part of me had grown into adulthood, it wasn't *all* of me. It was a tender moment when I touched the aspect of me that was acutely aware of when I was constricting into perfectionism and rigidity. Eventually, I began to learn how to self-correct lovingly and talk about my perfectionism without criticizing myself. I learned to put down my always-productive self, sit in silence, and clear away the debris of false beliefs that I was a failure or would be abandoned if I wasn't perfect. Simply, I started to learn I am human.

I began this journey of self-discovery after talking with a close friend whose heart had opened with the guidance of a woman named Moe. She said Moe helped people who wanted to find inner peace and a calmer way to live while still living in the chaos of the world. After learning more, I couldn't wait to get to Moe's place, nestled among the trees and rolling hills. It was there that my heart eventually opened and my own path of awakening was gradually revealed. Moe embraces people from all walks of life and faiths, as long as they want to accelerate their journeys. There are no set beliefs or dogmas—only a direct invitation to examine the beliefs and habits that cause separation from our true selves.

Never in my wildest dreams would I have imagined the significance of my first two-day intensive retreat and my ongoing journey with her. It was with her that my heart finally opened to life and something much bigger than me.

Moe's life coach lived with me for many months. As I started to live again, I thought of the people who aren't able to stay with their feelings, and who instead must go through their pain while heavily medicated. I knew one day I would revisit the luxury I had been given and pay it forward. As you will see in my ongoing journey, I did.

It Was Him

AFTER OUR FIRST MEETING, HE ASKED ME TO GO WITH HIM to the farthest part of the golf course and sit under a giant shade tree. We sat on the soft grass, close to one another, having met less than forty-eight hours before. He told me about his passion to live fully and to live up to his potential. He told me about how, when he was playing golf, he was in heaven. He didn't have to say it. I could see heaven on his face and in his eyes. I wanted heaven too. He had found his niche in life. It suited him well.

I loved watching his face light up when he told me he had won three English amateur titles and was considered the player most likely to succeed out of a large new crop of English professionals. He also told me how playing golf at Arizona State University had given him the opportunity to play among the best players in the collegiate league, where he became the best of the best.

As he spoke about his success, I noticed he didn't sound arrogant. He sounded proud. I learned that part of his pride came from knowing so many people had participated in his success. He expressed gratitude for his parents being relentless cheerleaders for their passionate young son. He spoke about the coaches who inspired him. His success was not just his own. It was very clear golf lived in the center of his heart.

When he explained the difference between the US and European tours, I became more and more mesmerized by his descriptions of the golf tournaments in Germany, Spain, and France. The excitement in his voice expressed how proud he was to be from England as he shared story after story. I entered further into his world. He told me about the courtesy cars granted to US players. In Spain, because the cars wouldn't fit on the streets, they rode bicycles. I listened to every word. My heart melted as I experienced his childlike excitement.

I wanted him to like me. I thought that if I shared more of my accomplishments, he would see me as a competent person, like him. When I told him I loved horses and excelled in competitive equestrian sports, his eyes lit up. I also told him about my love of interior design, travel, and adventure. The quiet moments and pauses between our various topics felt natural; however, I was more concerned about him liking me than telling him the exact truth. I made everything sound a little better than it was. I found the right words to paint a picture of a smart, athletic, independent, and feminine woman.

In those moments, I liked him and I liked me. It was simple, and we were tender. It had been a long time since I had sat on the grass under a tree. My life had become complicated. Being a college student and preparing to study in England and pursue my passion had been exhausting. It required my full attention. Wasn't something always pulling me away from moments like this? I was a doer, on the go, always trying to respond perfectly to a forward pull.

As we sat together, I remembered the innocence of my child-hood. I was redeeming something from a long time ago, when life wasn't so busy and my mind wasn't so full of an endless stream of thoughts. Under the shade of that tree, my mind quieted down; I listened with rapt attention to every word he said. I felt him listening to me. That is, until he said, "I am unwinding a relation-ship with a woman I have been with for a while. I want to get your number to put in my phone. I really want to get to know you."

I immediately felt the grip of fear and inadequacy when he mentioned another woman. Within seconds I started to add more paint to my human canvas of achievements, trying to make his view of me better and better. The quiet moments faded as my mind raced like a wild pony. I talked faster. I interrupted his sentences. I could feel my mind spinning and full of questions about the future, like, "When will I see you again?"

It was only years later that I understood. In the initial quiet with him, I was beginning to strip away layers of self-protection. As we were sharing, my heart was opening. I was feeling a glim-mer of inner peace. I was falling in love with him. However, it would be many years before I could fall in love with myself.

Once we parted, I didn't hear from him for two days as he traveled to Mexico for another tournament. It was torture. I couldn't think of anything else. I checked my phone every five minutes to see if I had missed the call. Golf was not necessarily a new world for me, as I was quite accomplished in my own right as an amateur athlete. I was well aware of the practice and dedi-cation it took, which also meant focusing on the game.

Nevertheless, I drove around in my dark blue Volvo with my windows rolled down, blasting sappy, romantic country music and feeling sorry for me. Maybe he wasn't breaking up with his girlfriend. Maybe I would never hear from him again. Maybe he'd lost my number. Maybe I should call *him*. Maybe he would find out I was not as independent and accomplished as I had led him to believe.

I was wrong. He did text me, and for two weeks we had the most beautiful interactions, most of the time while I was in class or lecture. My phone bill was a thousand dollars for the month I met him, due to the number of messages we sent back and forth. I felt so special. My heart skipped a beat every time I saw his name come up on my phone.

One day, my cell phone rang. "Hi, Jocelyn. I'm on my way to see you. I'm going to make it from Phoenix to Florida in twenty-four hours, so I will be at your apartment about two o'clock tomorrow morning." I swallowed my gasp and pulled myself together so he would have no idea I had been waiting by the phone. I was out-of-my-mind excited. I prepared my apartment as if a king were arriving.

Everything I was involved in came to a complete halt so I could appear absolutely perfect. I cleaned. I organized. I shaved my legs. I redid my hair and make-up. I adorned myself with carefully chosen clothes. I paced. My architect drafting table had never been so organized, nor my kitchen so immaculate. I did notice that he would be getting to see some of what I loved. My walls were filled with inspirational design interiors I had cut from magazines.

The day he was set to arrive, I skipped all my classes at Santa Fe College to be with him. I broke some rules, knowing love was overshadowing any of my own dreams. I loved it when he said, "You know, in England, for dinner sometimes we have a bottle of wine with a baguette and cheese." I loved our first kiss. He was tender and soft. I felt like I was in heaven and all was right with me and the world.

I remember thinking he was going to show me a whole new world full of travel and adventure. My heart was exploding and breaking down all the barriers I had created between me and life.

One morning, after an intimate, tender night, he made crepes for breakfast and introduced me to his favorite CD of British electronic music. As he was cooking, I told him more about my childhood home and farm. I had helped my dad build the barn and dig trenches when he was constructing our brick house with a huge front porch. He loved the thought of me working with farm equipment and suggested we go out and look at the tractors and mowers.

We jumped into his shiny black Volkswagen Jetta and headed to Home Depot, where the tractors were all lined up in a row. We must have looked so in love as we laughed hysterically and played with all the gears and different models. It had been a long time since I had played like this and laughed so hard. It felt like we had been transported to another planet. Is that what love does?

Next to the Home Depot was a Barnes and Noble, and we raced each other to the travel section and sat on the floor in the middle of the aisle, pulling out books about England. His smile got wider and wider as he turned pages, showing me everything about his homeland. I was mesmerized. He seemed so smart, well-traveled, cultured, and most of all, happy. When he told me his dad was South African, I was even more impressed. I told him that I wanted to travel the world. In that moment, our eyes locked. Nothing was said, but I knew I wasn't protecting my heart. Love was unleashing. I had never felt this way before.

When he had to leave for Arizona, we each shed tears. We didn't want to part, but he had to go back to his golf, and I had four more weeks of school to complete. All I could think about was him. School didn't feel important anymore. Without him, nothing felt important. When he called, whatever we talked about was all that mattered. In a matter of weeks, our relationship became more important to me than anything.

Reverse Course

I WAS OVER-THE-MOON IN LOVE. EVERYTHING IN LIFE FELT alive. I found myself being kinder to other people, laughing more, and I wanted to run down the street telling everyone I was in love.

I didn't think of much else as I was packing to move across the Atlantic Ocean. I knew my interest in attending design school was fading, but it wasn't until he met me in London that I knew I would rather live and travel with him than pursue my own interests. It wasn't long until he shared that he would love that too.

It was fast. I forgot about school, and we started living together.

Upon reflection, I now know this one decision was the beginning of me creating a false refuge. I was merging into his life and caught in a trance that would eventually divide us. It wasn't so much that continuing my education was wrong. It was more that I was counting on our love to be bigger than my own dreams and passions.

It would be many years before I learned my happiness could only be sustained by returning to the soft whispering of my true nature behind all the busy-ness in my world. As we journeyed together on the tour, the simple joy of sitting in the aisles of a bookstore became more and more distant. Eventually, we were sitting on verandas overlooking some of the most prestigious and beautiful golf courses in the world. I found myself learning more than I had ever expected and more than I had imagined.

While he was following a rigorous regimen with his golf practice, I returned to my familiar pattern of trying to do everything right so he would love me. I didn't know how to stop the cycle. Moment after moment, my mind replayed every interaction with everyone, highlighting how I could have said or done this or that better and differently. Instead of generously being concerned about others, my focus was on striving to shine in my new role of being a professional golfer's girlfriend.

I don't remember questioning the decision not to go to school, or even noticing it as an important departure from my real self until many years later. We were in love—or at least that's what I thought. I see now that I didn't love myself at that time. Our love and his comforting praises of me initially helped me feel relief from my fear and judgment of myself. As I said, my perfectionism registered as a quality he admired; he had no idea of the price I was paying in my heart for making everything for us "just right, all the time." He expressed appreciation for my extreme attention to detail, and I don't think either of us knew my desire to make him happy would lead me farther and farther away from my own dreams.

As we traveled the tour, I gradually learned how it all worked and what was needed to support him in being the best he could be. Just like I had wanted a pony to take care of as a young girl, I wanted to take care of him. More than anything, I wanted him to say, "Will you marry me?"

Looking back at this now, I see my insecurities. I had been living in a dualistic world: self and other, me and you, us and them. In those moments of sharing our dreams and stories under the shade of the tree, playing on the tractors, and making love, there was a humming voice in my head saying, "He will make me happy." At that time, I didn't know that other people can only contribute to my happiness. My happiness was already deep inside of me; I didn't know it. I had no clue I was beginning a journey from a place of neediness and longing for something on the outside to fill me up.

As I was falling in love, big chunks of me were underground. As I became familiar with his big world on the professional golf tour, my world felt smaller and smaller. He seemed so confident, and there was no way I was going to expose my uneasiness and self-doubts. I wanted him to fill that hole in my soul and connect me with life.

As we both felt the heat of new love, neither of us had any idea that I was walking away from my own dreams and desires. It was a long time before I learned that when I veered from a commitment to my vision, I wasn't as attractive to him. It gets worse—much worse.

Going for the Green

In May 2001, he played in the Benson and Hedges Tournament at the prestigious Belfry Golf Resort located north of Birmingham, England, near Coleshill. It was his first European Tour event. As our bank accounts were not overflowing with money, we stayed at a quaint little countryside hotel where our room was about the size of my closet at home. We were cozy, and that was all that mattered to either of us.

I was surprised they didn't have country clubs in Europe; they have golf resorts. On the drive through the English countryside, he told me all about this course, the Brabazon, where many famous golfers such as Seve Ballesteros and Nick Faldo had played and won. Some resorts in Britain have different names for the courses to commemorate certain events or people. In this case, the Brabazon course was named after the former PGA president, Lord Brabazon upon its opening in 1977.

I had never heard these names. He was very deliberate in

telling me that Seve was from Spain, and at age twenty-three had won the Masters and was a three-time winner of the British Open. Seve was as inspirational in Europe as Arnold Palmer was in America. Nick Faldo was one of the great English golfers. As he continued to share more about golfers and golf, I became more and more excited about being with him at the Belfry. I was also nervous.

This would be my first golf tournament as the girlfriend of a player. Ironing his light-blue shirts in our humble little hotel room, I felt as though I was playing an important role, and he thanked me a million times as I ironed them perfectly. While ironing, my mind raced forward to wondering what I was to do at the course while he played. There was little relief from all the questions surfacing about how to handle myself at this tournament in my new role. Not wanting him to have the slightest idea that I was insecure, I kept telling myself I would figure it out. I learned a lot about golfers, tournaments, and myself on this trip. I also told him I loved ironing his shirts and doing anything that would help him.

As we were packing up his Honda for a week on the road, I was amazed to learn how important shoe polish was to him. He was very particular about his shoes and always wanted them to be polished. He didn't want a high shine. He wanted a tip-top medium shine. Months later, I noticed a bit of dirt on his white shoes. I didn't want to cover it up with shoe polish, so I used a British version of Windex that he kept inside his car to clean his windows. I also used the barbecue brush he used to dust his car interior. I sprayed the white shoes with the cleaner and scrubbed them hard with the brush, hoping to get the dirt off. I was mortified when I saw the white leather chipping off. I quickly covered the area with white polish. He never noticed, thank God, but I was nervous.

In addition to the shoe polish, he also packed his golf clubs, rain gear, umbrellas, black-and-white shoes, changes of clothing, and personal items. I noticed he was meticulous in how he placed everything to make the best use of space. He was extremely organized, and of course I was too. I was careful not to take up too much space. I didn't want him to think I was one of those girls who would interfere in any way with his usual routines. This was so important to me that I remember not taking a few items of my own that I would have enjoyed having with me. I am sure he never knew about those things. Over and over again, I told him I was a real easy, light packer. Eventually that did become true, but only because I was trying not to make any kind of waves.

Upon arrival at the Belfry, we drove down the long driveway. The driving range was full of players and caddies preparing for the tournament. I wondered if we were late and quickly learned that wasn't his style. Being on time for everything was important to him and me. Fortunately, we weren't late. However, he started to quicken his pace. I kept up with him as we entered the registration office to let the officials know he had arrived and to get the yardage book outlining the markers for the course. In this registration office, I experienced the background operation that made the tournament tick like clockwork.

When we arrived at the registration building, located at the back of the historical clubhouse covered in thick ivy, he turned me around and pointed me towards the tenth hole. He said, "This is the hole that can win the tournament." I so desperately wanted him to win. The tenth hole was special for many reasons, but mainly for its risk/reward possibility. A player could either go for the green from the tee and possibly make eagle, or hit his tee shot in the fairway and have a tricky shot to the green. Water surrounded the green, which automatically made it scary. Needless to say, he showed me his fearless yet calculated approach, and I saw exactly how one "goes for the green."

After registering, we walked back to the car, where we met his new caddy, Stuart Dryden, a very seasoned Australian. Stu had a gentle persona and was kind to me. I sensed he knew this was my first time behind the scenes of a tournament. He must have read my body language; I was nervous and stiff as a board. It was also his first time to meet Stu face-to-face after hiring him. It didn't take long for him to know they were a great match.

Looking around at my new world, I felt like I was riding a roller coaster on shaky tracks. It was a familiar feeling. I vacillated between the comforting thought that I could fit right into his world and my self-tormenting questions: Did I look okay? Was I saying the "right" things as he introduced me to his friends? Would I be accepted by these beautiful people? Yikes. This was nerve-wracking.

I would like to say I didn't notice what the golf wives and/or significant others looked like, but I did. I noticed every detail from their hairstyle and makeup to their jewelry and outfits—and. of course, their shoes. For the next ten years while traveling on the tours, I continued to notice. I compared myself. I wanted her bag, her shoes, her full lips, her hair, her curvy figure. Comparing myself to the other women became another inner roller coaster. I hated myself for it. Prior to the tours, I had noticed other women's styles because I was curious and interested. Gradually, I quietly started to compare myself to most of the women I was meeting. The competition between us was never talked about. As I matured, I longed to talk about it. Crafting the perfect image for him and the media was exhausting. The snake was once again looming in the crevices of every conversation.

Stu was older and experienced on the tours. It was a chilly, rainy, overcast day, and he wanted to get to the driving range and start hitting balls. I almost commented on the chill, but kept my mouth shut because I didn't want to appear as if I was complaining.

Later, I learned he liked to walk the course before a tournament. Sometimes I walked with him, in silence, as he carefully studied the terrain and visualized playing on the course; other times he talked about the layout and design. I was very careful to gauge what he needed. If he was silent, I was silent. If he talked about golf or the course, I listened. I tried to never, ever, take up any space or irritate him.

For the first two days at the Belfry, I simply walked the sidelines of the course, watching Stu and him working together. While it might have appeared I was completely present for every move he was making, I wasn't. Once again, a million entangled thoughts were racing through my head. The course was stunningly beautiful. He was perfect. Yet there I was, wondering if I was doing it right.

My sister and I were both accomplished golfers but this was different. Now I was seeing my new life unfolding. I wasn't familiar with only watching others play, and something was being stirred up in me. I had no clue what it was. I felt out of sorts.

On the third day, I finally decided to sit on the gorgeous, expansive stone terrace rather than walk the course. The rectangular gold pin with the European Tour logo on my shirt lapel meant I could go anywhere I wanted. It signified I was with a player. I ordered some toast with my coffee, and while watching the players hitting balls on the putting green, my mind zigzagged everywhere.

I hadn't met any of the players' wives or girlfriends, and I wondered if they were going to come over to me and say hello. Maybe they were friends with his former girlfriend. He had confessed he and his former girlfriend had talked about marriage, so maybe the wives weren't sure of my role. I wasn't quite sure yet either. I hated not knowing. I wanted a map. I wanted it to be clear that I was with *him*. I hated sitting there alone with a million story lines running through my head. The questions and thoughts kept bombarding any enjoyment I could have had at this gorgeous place with the love of my life. I was missing it all with my constant worry, insecurity, and pride.

I tried to act like I was fine sitting there eating my toast. No one came over to me and said hello. I could hear laughter. Once again, I was on the periphery of the conversations. At that time, it didn't even occur to me to walk over to the women and introduce myself. I was insulated in a capsule named "All About Me." Would they like me? It was all about me.

On the fourth day, Thursday, the tournament started. He played well; he shot a 69. Finally, I was more focused on his success than my self-doubts. He finished the tournament in twelfth place.

As we drove home, he told me he could have done better. As he processed his shots out loud, I listened. I didn't try to rescue him by telling him he was great. I asked questions but barely listened to his answers. He was reviewing his game while I was thinking about where I was going to get my hair cut. I realized he didn't know I wasn't listening when he reached over to hold my hand. I loved that, of course. I was a good faker.

He also informed me we would be flying to Heidelberg, Germany, for the Deutsche Bank Tournament (TPC) the very next week. His mind was moving forward, and so was mine. I was excited to go to Germany. However, there were shirts to iron, clothes to wash, and bags to pack before the next journey. I was beginning to wonder about my own clothes, but apparently not enough to prevent a little scene when we arrived.

Tournament After Tournament

I HAD ON A PAIR OF WHITE, BACKLESS SNEAKERS WHEN WE arrived at St. Leon Rot, Heidelberg Golf Club—Germany's premier golf tournament and one of the game's richest competitions. It was raining, and I clearly wasn't prepared. One of the ladies in the registration area came up to me and said, "Oh, you have on the wrong shoes to be out here." My heart sank. I was the embarrassing girlfriend. He explained to the woman that it would be okay because I wouldn't be out there long. I was relieved and had fun walking the course with Wayne Riley, a comical and outgoing Australian player.

Later, I was merciless with myself for this little incident. Why hadn't I known this? Why had I worn those shoes? Why hadn't I paid attention? My body became tighter and tighter as I beat myself up for this mistake. My biggest concern was that I had embarrassed him and he was going to break up with me. I tried to stop the thoughts, but they kept coming like a swift-moving train. No matter what I did to distract myself, the fear of failure loomed behind every distraction. The only thing that helped me was gaining more and more control of my environment.

As we traveled from city to city, hotel to hotel, it was important to me to arrange our hotel rooms to feel as much like home as possible. Initially, we couldn't afford the hotels on the grounds of the tournaments, as they were too expensive. I longed to stay in the nicer places, but I recognized that as long as I stayed with him, we would one day have the money to stay wherever we wanted. In the meantime, I wanted every hotel room to feel homey, especially since we usually stayed in them for six days. I wanted to show off my interior design skills and prove to him that I would do everything possible to make his life perfect.

When we checked in, his standard question was, "Okay, so what are you going to do this time?" It was my go sign to get to work. I put away all the little cardboard signs that said things like *Give us your recommendations* and *If you want to reuse your towel more than once.* If the furniture was movable and not positioned for our comfort, I shifted it all around. I loved paying attention to what he liked and didn't like. I made the room just as he wanted.

I carefully unpacked our bags, organizing everything the way he liked it, drawer by drawer. Along with stylish, polished shoes, clean socks were a necessity. One time we stayed in a place that did not have a washing machine. I was so irate that I wrote the manager a letter and complained. Nothing was going to stop me from meeting his needs.

I am not sure he was aware of how much I was doing for him, because I didn't always let him know. Honestly, he would have died that I was angry with the manager for not having a washing machine. He was far more polite than I was at that time.

He always picked out his clothes the evening before. While he was taking his morning shower, I carefully laid out the chosen clothes in the order he would be putting them on, so he wouldn't have to think about anything but golf.

At this time, even I wasn't aware of the amount of energy I was using to please him. It wasn't so much physical energy as emotional energy. I remember spreading his clothes out on the bed, then stepping back and looking at each item to make sure everything was perfect. It took many years for me to realize the price I was paying to *take care* of someone rather than *caring for* him. Yuck. I so didn't want to be that girl, but I was.

Serial Perfectionism

THE SCENARIO CONTINUED FOR THE FIRST THREE YEARS I traveled with him on tour. While he introduced me to every aspect of the golf world, I remained on the periphery, trapped in self-doubt. Much like a moth on a sweater, snuggling close to what felt comfortable in the cold winter months, I stayed close to him or was alone. I spent a lot of time alone.

Even as young girl, I loved being alone. I can't remember a single time when I felt lonely. It was easy and blissful to spend hours in my bedroom, creating my own idea of a shop selling unique clothing and furniture. I would carefully place every item for maximum design impact and use of space. I loved hanging my special dress from the ceiling fan. I took pride in knowing many details about my furniture and all the items I was selling to the imaginary customers who walked into the shop. My brain was flooded with innovative ideas. I created a drive-through window for people who wanted to shop from the comfort of their cars. My vintage school desk held a cash register and Monopoly money. This was a serious operation. I loved the interactions with my customers. I would often teach them how the furniture was made and the history of their purchases. I remember long discussions about the texture of the chair fabric and how confident I felt knowing these details.

I was alone in my own world and in complete control. The grinding chatter and noise in the world faded. I was propelled into a world where creativity was uncensored and unleashed.

As I matured, creating alone time to move from one idea to the next was not so easy. Gradually I became caught up in the frantic rat race of getting things done, being efficient, being responsible, and of course, in my case, being perfect. As a young girl, it was easy for me to carve out space when no one could interfere with my wild, creative mind. I loved it. I wasn't self-conscious. Traveling on the tour was different. While he practiced, I accomplished all of the tasks needed to keep us perfectly organized. I tried to anticipate his every need. My mind roamed between the past and the future.

Sometimes I ventured out alone from the tournament to explore new places, sounds, and smells. I loved finding off-the-beaten-path restaurants, little bookstores, and clothing shops. I also loved walking in crowded city environments where I felt bathed in colors, texture, architecture, foreign languages, and culture. When I returned from my journey, we would meet and share the events of the day. He was happy when I was happy. He was interested in where I had been.

It took a long time to learn that when I was alone and making my own way, I felt free of my perfectionism. That was until the time I became lost in Cologne, Germany. I walked for miles in this vibrant city before I realized I couldn't find my way back to the Dorint Kongress Hotel. We stayed there while he was playing in the Linde German Masters Tournament. I was bone-tired and more than frustrated that I had lost my sense of direction in this city.

I noticed a group of German students standing near a bus stop, and I wanted to ask them how to get back the hotel. They looked approachable. But something made me hesitate to walk up to them and ask for help. That "something" was familiar. We could call it many different names, but I knew the truth. It was my perfectionism. I called it "serial perfectionism." I didn't want anyone to think I wasn't perfect or that I needed help with *anything.*

I made note of how pathetic I felt. Then I took a deep breath and asked the students how to get back to the hotel. It was a shock to learn that I had already walked right past it three times. I couldn't laugh. I was angry with myself for not paying attention. It upset me to realize I had allowed such a narrow margin for error. I was too embarrassed to tell him at dinner that I had been lost and had to ask for help. Instead, I faked it.

He seemed so perfect. When he made mistakes, he laughed.

Magnificent Mile

As you might expect, I was starting to feel exhausted from the enormous weight of my "serial perfectionism." With each golf tournament and each event, the weight seemed to get heavier.

I had seen Caroline Harrington out of the corner of my eye during many tournaments. I noticed her stunning beauty and poised manner. She was married to Padraig Harrington, an Irish golfer who played on both the European and the PGA tours. He told me Padraig and Caroline seemed to have a great marriage, and that's when I knew I wanted to meet her. As you know by now, it wasn't my way to initiate a meeting, but we did finally meet in southern Spain when the Volvo Masters was held at Valderrama Golf Club. It had been rated the top course in mainland Europe in 1999 by *Golf World* magazine.

Caroline and Padraig were eating breakfast at a table near us when I overheard their wonderful Irish accents. We were introduced, and I instantly liked her. She asked if I would like to join her by the pool along with Sandra Price, the spouse of Phillip Price from Wales. Despite knowing I might not look so great in my bathing suit after eating not one, but two croissants at breakfast, I said yes. There was something about Caroline that helped me feel comfortable. I was curious about her. I later learned she was known for her immaculate, runway-perfect makeup and hair, and her ability to handle the media and crowds with grace, kindness, and appreciation. I knew I also possessed these qualities. My parents had taught me well. But I wanted to express them naturally, like Caroline did.

As I sat by the pool in sunny southern Spain with a hint of olive tree scent in the air, for a brief moment I didn't feel self-conscious. These women were real, and I think authenticity is contagious. I could feel they were comfortable with themselves, and I wanted to feel that way too. I made myself enter in the conversation rather than stay on the periphery.

We ordered all sorts of fabulous food, and Caroline and Sandra told me about their Ryder Cup experiences. I was fascinated with both women. I did not realize this small gathering was the beginning of me partaking in more activities with the women traveling on the tours.

Later, I learned that golf clubs and resorts wanted to lure the guys to play at their clubs, especially the big-name professionals. They offered the golfers' ladies luncheons and shopping trips. I had never attended any of these activities until Caroline asked me to go with her on the shopping trip. It was offered at the US Open in the summer of 2003 at Olympia Fields Country Club, outside of Chicago. At first I didn't want to go, but remembering how comfortable I was with her, I said yes.

All of the wives going on the trip gathered outside the golf course clubhouse and waited for a chartered bus. From the moment I arrived, I felt self-conscious and insecure. At this time I didn't wear many designer clothes and certainly didn't carry an expensive purse. I loved high quality, classic, practical clothing. I couldn't help but compare myself to the other women waiting. I came up short in every category.

These women looked like a group of perfectly mannered, manicured models hired to wear diamonds, shoes, and designer outfits from an ultra-high-end, exclusive boutique. I felt *too simple*. I wanted to run back to my hotel room. Instead, as we boarded the bus, I signaled to Caroline to join me in sitting in the farthest back seat.

As we traveled to Chicago's Magnificent Mile, Caroline assured me we would have the opportunity to shop in fabulous department stores. Caroline was already established on the tour, and she was comfortable with the group. As each tall, thin, tan woman boarded, I sank deeper in my seat. Caroline started chatting amicably as I was about to bolt back to my room to sulk. I was mortified that I had not brought the money necessary to shop on the Magnificent Mile. If we had been headed to an equestrian shop, I would have known what to expect.

Caroline shared that many of the women loved to shop at Saks Fifth Avenue. Often, in addition to purchasing things for themselves, they bought gifts for their husbands. I couldn't even imagine what I might buy for him other than another blue shirt or white socks or shoe polish. We hadn't bought expensive items for each other, and I was rapidly becoming very aware of that fact.

As Caroline spoke, I noticed her beautiful jewelry. When I complimented her, she told me that every time Padraig won a tournament, she was invited to choose a piece of jewelry for herself. I wanted that too, and more.

Just as I was starting to forget that my hair, makeup, outfit, shoes, purse, watch, and jewelry weren't even a close comparison to what these women were wearing, it got worse. A tall, gorgeous, veteran wife stood up next to the bus driver, pulled out a microphone, and with her sparkling-forever, diamond-fingered hands, signaled that she wanted each of us to introduce ourselves. We were to say who we were married to. I thought I was going to pass out from fear. I was mortified. Caroline reassured me that by the time they got to the back of the bus, we would probably be at Saks and I wouldn't have to do it.

As each woman stood up, I could feel my throat closing. I couldn't listen to these women speak as my hands were trembling. I looked outside to see if we were near our destination, but I had no clue where we were. I don't know how I did it, but when it was my turn I stood up, I said I was Jocelyn, his girlfriend. Then I sat down so quickly, I don't remember if I even said anything else. All I knew was that it was over. I wanted to throw up.

Our time on the Magnificent Mile was okay, but by no means magnificent. I held my own but didn't buy anything. I also made sure I didn't look in any mirrors. Have you ever noticed how many mirrors are in some department stores? I felt like some of them were saying, "Come over here and look at you. You don't belong with these women." I was so tired of tearing myself down, I didn't want to make it any worse.

I knew I had to make some big changes to keep up with these women. For the first time that I could remember, I wanted to. I started to think I could love this lifestyle a lot—a whole lot. This event was my entry into the world of designer-name clothes, shoes, jewelry, and purses. I picked up a purse and looked at it carefully, loving it. When I saw the $15,000 price tag, I wanted it.

As I look back now, I wonder how different this feeling was from that of teenager who wants to fit in during junior high. I rapidly descended into a world of extreme consumerism. I wanted to open up my closet to the clothes and shoes and purses and jewels that would signal I belonged.

Growing up, I was fortunate to have abundance. I had clothes and a lifestyle that other girls my age envied. My family traveled. We ate at expensive restaurants. We had a beautiful home, property, and horses. If I had wanted expensive jewelry or an expensive purse, I am sure I could have gotten it.

The difference between my youth and my experience on the bus was that as a young girl, I chose the clothes I wore based on what I loved, not on what would make me fit in. I didn't compare myself to others. Though I wanted to be perfect, I wanted to be perfect by my own standards. On the bus, it was others' standards that I aspired to.

I don't want to give the impression that the tour wives compared themselves to each other. All I know is that my hypercritical self-examination on the bus was a torture I will never forget. I arrived back at the hotel starved for some sort of validation. I don't remember what I did to try to impress him, but I am quite sure I did something big. I was becoming a master manipulator.

Comparing ourselves to each other and feeling better or less than seems to be an epidemic among American women—or maybe all over the world. I do know I am powerless against the raging, jealous fires that can burn into my bones. In my healing, I have talked with many women about jealousy. I am not alone. Every woman I have spoken with has shared the same torment. How can we feel so confident in one moment, then see another woman who seems to be more in every way, and suddenly feel like a puddle on the floor?

I asked Moe about jealousy of other women. I will never forget what she said: "My dear. When you feel jealous of another woman, lean into her. Get to know her. Learn from her. Don't run away. The jealousy will pass. Just learn from her. Always know in your heart that women truly do want to help each other. It is not our nature to compete in this way. We are hand holders. You are not likely to be jealous of a woman who doesn't have something to teach you." I will never forget this reply. I carry many pearls of wisdom that I received from Moe within me to this day.

Silence

GRADUALLY, I BECAME MORE AWARE OF THE ACHING IN MY heart. I was angry at myself for not being perfect. Because of my hypercriticism, self-doubt, and overmanagement of his life, I started to feel depleted. I don't remember the exact day or the time, but I do remember recognizing that something was wrong the day I was curled up in a soft burgundy velvet chair. I was attempting to read a magazine article a friend had sent to me, but I only looked at the photos. I had always looked forward to quiet time, but I was too restless to read the article.

Finally, I put the magazine down. I tried eating a peach and watching the Golf Channel, but none of my usual diversions helped. He was out on the course with Stu. I had a spa appointment scheduled for three o'clock. I was living the American Dream, and yet something wasn't right. Everyone else seemed content and happy. I felt empty.

Finally, I flopped down on the huge hotel bed, feeling an

overwhelming sense of sadness. Eventually, my eyes wandered over to the big picture window with the distant view of the expansive blue sky. I remembered the times when, as a young girl, I couldn't go to sleep because I was too excited for the morning light to make its way into my bedroom. I wanted to run out to the stable and see my pony. Soft tears streamed down my cheeks as I awakened to the truth that I hadn't been excited about anything for a very long time. Something big was missing in my life.

I tried to push away these feelings of sadness by rearranging the room and continuing with my travel routine. I told myself to be grateful for the extraordinary life I was living, but self-talk wasn't working.

I especially remember a rainy morning when we were eating pancakes in a sweet café with another golfer and his wife. I joined in the conversation, but my thoughts were a million miles away. The three of them talked about how the sleeting rain was going to affect that day's tournament while I drifted back to a time when I was on my horse cantering through an open field.

As I was hanging on for dear life in my little daydream, the waitress asked me if I wanted strawberry or maple syrup. Startled that I had drifted so far away from reality, I knew that something had to change. That moment carried me a long way into my life.

I wanted to talk with someone about this, but I couldn't think of one person who would understand, even my sister. Almost all of my friends were envious of my life. Any complaint from me wasn't sincerely tolerated. I lost contact with many of the friends I used to cherish. Traveling on the tour was a full-time job. Between trips, we planned and prepared for the next one.

Over and over I asked myself why traveling on tour with such a wonderful man wasn't enough. After all, I was living a life of luxury many women only dreamed about. I was with not only a successful man, but a kind man. As he became more successful, we traveled on private jets or in first class on commercial flights. I drove expensive cars, shopped in high-end clothing stores, and purchased almost anything I had ever wanted.

I wondered if he could tell I wasn't happy. I tried to act like everything was okay, but I knew there would come a time when I could no longer stuff the truth. I missed my horses. I missed my dream of becoming an interior designer. I knew I had to talk to him about this, but I was afraid—mostly afraid he would think the horses and my own career desires were more important to me than him. I was afraid if I told him my heart was aching for my own successes and failures, everything would come to a sudden halt. I couldn't bear the thought of not being with him or of hurting him. I wanted to spend the rest of my life with him.

I stood in front of the bathroom mirror to practice what I wanted to say. I wanted every word to be expressed perfectly. I waited for the right time. The right timing for athletes is critical. If I tried to talk to him prior to a tournament, I was afraid it might upset him. If he didn't do well on the course, I needed to wait. If he played well, I wanted to celebrate. I didn't want to be a downer talking about my needs or me. It was complicated.

As I reflect back on this inner turmoil, there was no real basis for me to be so nervous to talk with him about my dreams. The whisper of "if you are not by his side, someone else will be" continued to haunt me. I was terrorized by the thought of losing him and unable to talk about what I wanted.

For a long while, I continued to fake it. We humans are pretty good at that. I later learned that symptoms were starting to show up. Mine showed up as feeling exhausted, distant, and depressed. The storyline that I saw in my mind's eye was of a beautiful and better woman coming into his life. She would say the right things to him, and she would be warm and intimate, with engaging stories he hadn't already heard. What if? I couldn't allow that to happen.

I often wondered if any of the other tour women had this concern. There were many adoring girls at the events, and some of them were very bold about their desire to get an autograph, a smile, or any attention from one of the professional golfers. I was in a coveted position. Every time I looked at other females, I thought I came up short.

These thoughts and fears surfaced like a flash flood. I wanted to tell him, but I always stopped myself. I don't think either one of us had ever told the other we were insecure or afraid or needing help with anything. We were never vulnerable with each other. We didn't open the door to our humanness. I think some people might have viewed our relationship as "polite." We didn't argue. We were painfully silent unless we were talking about golf and the tour.

Opening the Door

FINALLY, I COULDN'T HOLD IT ANYMORE. IN THE WINTER of 2003, the right moment appeared, and I told him about my wanting to reenter the worlds of equestrian competition and interior design. He looked relieved. I didn't know what that meant at the time, but he was clearly not only supportive but happy. I headed for the barn.

I couldn't wait to slip into my German-made, form-fitting Pikeur breeches with beautiful suede patches inside the knees. My zip-up, black, custom Italian riding boots wrapped around my legs like melted butter. When I was in my boots, I felt at home; I felt like the person I knew.

With his encouragement, after nearly two and a half years of witnessing his success, I started to win horse competitions again. I became known for being more than his partner. I entered competitions and traveled with my barn team: fifteen women with my kind of passion. I can't tell you how much fun we had planning and packing our wooden tack trunks with our gear. The months we went to Canada were beyond fun.

The horse shows in British Columbia were among our favorites because of the intense competition and derby-style showing. Derby shows consist of jumping over dry ditches and banks, which our horses were not exactly accustomed to. We were pushed beyond our limits. I loved every moment and was feeling alive again.

We became a tightly knit team. We arrived at the show stables before the sun came up, carrying enormous bags of carrots and looking like little girls with their ponies. Most of us competed in the same classes, so we would slip on our boots and get to the show ring to study the course design. We walked the course together with steaming cups of coffee in our hands and horsehair all over our jackets. This was where I felt at home. I felt free. No one could remove the happiness I felt in my heart.

As I entered more and more competitions, both my confidence and skills increased. In Canada, I was reserve champion in my division. I jumped higher in the 1.20 meter division. It was the highest I had ever wanted to jump, as long as I was doing it well. Show jumping required skill and mindfulness, and I loved testing the boundaries within myself.

He was there to witness it all, and the smile on his face reflected his happiness for my achievements. I was back in my element. I wasn't small. I was again the girl he had first met. I knew he loved me that day.

I often joked that if there were a candle that smelled like horsehair, dirt, and manure, I would buy it and travel around with it to feel close to my beloved horses. I loved arriving at the barn as the sun was rising, when the horses' breaths were visible in the early morning mist.

However, I also wondered if I had made a mistake in signing

up for competitions. I felt torn. I was accustomed to being on the golf course, where my "real job" was taking care of him. Despite his encouragement to continue to excel with my horses, I persistently worried about another woman walking toward him. She would be new, different, exciting, and beautiful. I decided I better travel more with him.

Abu Dhabi Decadence

WHILE I WAS HELPING HIM PACK FOR A TOURNAMENT IN Abu Dhabi, the capital of and second most populous city in the United Arab Emirates, I spontaneously decided to go with him. I canceled my horse competition. He was surprised but seemed happy. I knew that if I didn't accompany him, I would go crazy thinking about him being in such a beautiful, exotic place without me.

As I said good-bye to my sweet horses before departing, my heart felt like it was splitting in two. I felt far away from them as we boarded the flight to London. As I looked down from my first-class seat, my eyes flooded with tears. I glanced at him and felt deep love, but I also felt I was leaving what ultimately made me the happiest. I hid my tears, took a deep breath, and reminded myself that he came first. I tried to accept that my horses were a hobby. My real job was to take care of him. I told myself to never forget that or "she" would take him away.

The Abu Dhabi Golf Championship was very different from any other event I had attended. We were treated like royalty. We were flown first class on Etihad Airways, picked up by a luxurious private car, and escorted to a special VIP arrival hall, where we were whisked through immigration. Another chauffeur was waiting, and our luggage had already been carefully placed in a 7 series BMW.

We were taken to the Emirates Palace. We didn't check in; instead we were graciously greeted by the manager and escorted to our room. A butler, dressed in a black-and-white tuxedo, assured us that if we needed anything, day or night, he would get it for us. The smell of fresh lavender was intoxicating and everywhere. As we entered our enormous suite, he made a joke about being able to hit a full wedge from the living room to the bathroom. We were like two kids in a candy store with a hundred bucks and no rules.

Orchid petals adorned the gold bathtub. Extra-large, white, fluffy towels were stacked outside the enormous tiled shower. Gorgeous soft sheets covered the bed, twice as big as a king-size American bed. He smiled when he saw the ninety-inch television screen offering international stations. The living room was filled with magnificent hand-carved furniture and a fruit tray the size of a breakfast buffet. We were immersed in a level of decadence that neither of us had ever experienced.

While he practiced, I stayed inside and roamed the hallways. The decor was designed to reflect the elegance of the hotel; it took me one full hour to walk from one end to the other. Not only was the palace vast, but so was the restaurant menu. There was something for everyone. The Japanese were offered rice and fish; the Germans, bread and cheese with ham; and Americans could get eggs, bacon, and toast. The English could have baked beans on toast and spotted dick—a steamed, log-shaped suet pudding studded with currants. It's not very tasty in my opinion, but it is served in every pub in England. I felt like a member of the royal family. Whatever I needed was there in an instant.

The golf course was one of his favorites, representing several wins throughout his career. The players' lounge was lined with windows, making the eighteenth green comfortably visible. The clubhouse was shaped like a falcon, the coveted bird of the United Arab Emirates. Everything was immaculate and pristine and gorgeous.

He knew I would be missing my horses, so he surprised me with tickets to an FEI (Federation Equestre Internationale) World Cup qualifier. I was beyond excited. I invited Ulrika Stenson, the sister of a highly accomplished professional golfer and personal friend, Henrik Stenson. Ulrika was also a competitive show jumper, so we always had something to talk about. We loved touring the barn aisles, where we saw the horses of Sheika Latifa Al Maktoum. Sheika Latifa is the daughter of His Highness Sheikh Mohammed bin Rashed Al Maktoum, the prime minister of the United Arab Emirates. We were in awe being so close to the horses of such royalty and not surprised they were treated like little kings and queens. So were we.

Anything he organized was first class, as evidenced when I was honored by being given a jacket only worn by the Abu Dhabi Show Jumping Team. Watching the competition was inspiring, and I felt fire in my heart to compete and excel. As we flew back to the United States, my heart soared thinking about heading west for the summer and touring horse shows in the Pacific Northwest and Canada.

Love

EVENTUALLY, HE STARTED TO TAKE AN INCREASING INTEREST in watching my competitions and training. He purchased a Canon Mark II 5D with a mega zoom to take photos of everyone at the barn—but mainly me and our horses. He hated the thought of not being able to remember such beautiful memories. Everyone at Twisted Tree Farm was a huge fan of his, not only for his golf skills, but for the way he treated me.

I would routinely warm up in the ring before a class, and often he would surprise me. Out of the corner of my eye, I would see him standing at the side, quietly holding the camera, water, and carrots for the horses. I wondered if he could feel my appreciation for his support. It was real. But I had a feeling I wasn't showing much warmth to him, or to anyone for that matter. I had been braced and protecting my heart for so long that I wasn't sure how to express the love I felt for him.

Though he needed to practice, many times he stayed a little

longer at the barn. I wondered if he noticed I was warmer to the horses than to him. I didn't want to be, but I felt more inner peace and calm in the horse barn than anyplace on earth. I didn't feel a need to be perfect at the barn. I loved sitting in a stall while the horses licked my hand. I wished I could express the same love for him. I did love him, but it was scary to love him. My horses weren't going to leave me, and he might.

When I reflected on my increasing difficulty in expressing my truest feelings to him, I saw how I had been this way most of my life. I could only go so far before I tightened up. I wanted to be different. I wanted to be the girl with love overflowing from her heart. I wanted to express this love not only to him, but to everyone—to humans, not just to my horses.

Words weren't necessary with horses. I expressed myself to them by combing their manes, giving them carrots, and cleaning their stalls. It was simple. I felt a sense of partnership with all the horses in the barn. They were different from humans. They weren't always predictable, but they were controllable. They didn't judge me or ask for too much, and I could count on them. No one was going to take them away. They were safe.

I wanted that with him and other people, but I had seen relationships end too many times. My parents had divorced after being married for twenty-three years. I was thirteen years old when I learned that relationships can end in the blink of an eye. I didn't want that to happen to us. I was willing to do anything to make sure I was not going to be left alone. I wondered what it would take to guarantee his approval, acceptance, and love only for me, forever, no matter what.

The Moth Crawls Out of the Sweater

I DECIDED IT MIGHT HELP ME IF I TRIED TO GET TO KNOW more women on tour. It had been some time since that trip on the bus to the Magnificent Mile. I had watched Caroline pay sincere attention to each person. I saw how much she seemed to love being with the tour wives. I don't know if she was interested in everyone, but it sure looked like it. Simply, I wanted to be like her. I wanted to be around her and others like her. I felt that if I could learn to express myself to women, eventually I could express more love to him.

I was determined to be less of a moth nestled in a sweater, and to interact with more people. Just as I had watched Caroline's actions closely, I began to watch the wives and girlfriends interact. Because I never knew who was going to be at the tournaments, I saw a revolving circle of different women in various scenarios. I noticed how much they talked about their children, nannies, and relationships with their husbands. It is no secret that professional athletes can be difficult to live with. Often, it seemed that the needs and desires of the wives were secondary to golf.

As I leaned closer into friendships with the other women, I shared my passion for horses and competition. I was told time and time again how lucky I was to have an outlet of my own. They envied that I was able to come and go as I pleased. We talked about how hard it was to remain silent after a bad round or to admit a mistake if we forgot a badge in the hotel room. Given a professional golfer's laser-beam focus, we all agreed that they didn't forget very much or make silly mistakes. One tiny mistake—or what they perceived to be a mistake—could set them off.

I increased my time at the gym to get into better shape. I quietly compete not only with myself, but also with the other women. Exercise had always been an essential part of my day. Every day of my young life, I lifted heavy machinery, saddles, and tack, so naturally my muscles took shape and I liked it. I felt healthy and strong on the outside. I was the only girl in my fifth grade class who did thirty-two pull-ups. That was about twenty-nine more than anyone else. I never put anyone down for not being able to do as many as I did; if anything, I downplayed my ability to make them feel more comfortable. I can see now where this trait became a common thread in the fabric of my life.

As my time on tour continued, the gym was often my main activity. He was dedicated to his time in the gym; not one day was ever missed. I followed his footsteps. Many times we were alone in the gym except for Elin Woods, who was always there and usually on mile ten of her treadmill routine by the time we arrived. Working out was becoming a cultural trend, however, and eventually the gym was packed full of players and personal trainers.

Desiring perfection, I sought an introduction to Extreme Training in Scottsdale. My friend Jackie took me there, and when she mentioned she burned a thousand calories in one hour, I was hooked. Gradually, I entered a zone of exercise addiction. I wanted to be as slim and trim as possible and pushed myself as far as I could go. I wanted to control more in my life, and I could control my weight and exercise routine.

My first training session was awful and wonderful. I was told to drink three liters of water the day prior and to show up at 7:00 a.m. I drank 3.5 liters and arrived at six fifty. I had always been an early riser, mainly because my spinning mind woke me up. The studio was heated to one hundred degrees, which was part of the extreme nature of the program. We did sixty minutes of nonstop cardio with weights. I was certain I would throw up. Thank God I didn't.

I participated in this class six days a week for about six months when I was in Scottsdale. The last few years of our relationship, I was home more often and on the road less, so focusing on my own fitness was easy. My addiction progressed. I paid attention to every cut in each of my muscles. Everyone stared at me in awe and amazement. Predictably, I downplayed their compliments.

When I stood in front of the floor-to-ceiling mirrors, I was able to see the fruits of my hard work. I had a six-pack; my arms were ripped; my legs were as toned as a supermodel's. I was fit and in control … so I thought.

Later, in my healing journey, my strict fitness regimen began to feel less important. I was more interested in strengthening my inner guidance, not my biceps, inner thighs, and abs. I walked my dogs more, jogged a little here and there, and hiked. I see now how I blocked my ability to receive inner guidance while loud music was blaring. I sweated nearly two gallons of water every thirty minutes while obsessing about whether or not I was going to throw up. Anything extreme is, for me, not a path aligned with my inner compass. I now move away from anything of that nature. I respect those who do take part, but extreme anything concerns me.

It took me a long time to want to be in nature, or to care as much about my inner life as my outer life. I learned a definition of addiction that makes sense to me: anything you do that creates problems in your life, despite which you continue to do it, is likely to be addictive. When I was so focused on my outer self, I had no idea of the long-term negative effects. In many ways, as you will see, it had to get worse before it got better.

I cared more and more about what I was wearing. I shopped in better stores. I spent more money on pretty much everything that I thought would help me look better. I spent more time in front of the mirror, adjusting this or that. I looked in magazines to learn the latest styles and designers. Most of all, I was thinking about me, me, and me.

Just as he competed in golf to qualify for the Ryder Cup, I competed to be known as someone special among the golf wives. I wanted to shine. Because I couldn't always "win" in the beauty department—believe me, many tour wives are extraordinarily gorgeous—I tried to shine in different ways. I was genuinely proud of my equestrian achievements; as a young girl, I had taught myself to ride and take care of my horses without anyone's help. I was humble when I spoke of my passion. I knew I hadn't figured it all out, but that's always the case with sports. There is always more to be learned. During walks with the other women, I would share my love and enthusiasm for competing with my horses and traveling all over the world.

I wanted to purchase investment horses for resale and manage a small breeding operation in Germany. All the girls loved to hear about that. They asked me to keep talking forever. When a new foal arrived each spring, I asked the person I was with at the time to give me her favorite name for a horse. Elin Woods named my second foal, Caesar, while in Miami at Doral for the WGC event. It was fun. I felt like I was someone other than his wife. Beneath my increasingly cold and distant stance was a girl who wanted to fit in and be married, who was scared that she wasn't enough, despite the fact that everywhere we went, we were noticed.

There was no question that being with him carried status. When we walked into many restaurants, especially in Scottsdale and London, people noticed us. When we walked through airports, strangers tried to talk to him. If they couldn't capture his attention, they settled for mine. I remember one man wanted to know what kind of coffee he drank! I was often told I was fortunate to be with such a great man. I tried to be kind and to remember he was a public hero.

For a long time I enjoyed the doors that opened as a result of our status. Previously full restaurants suddenly had the best table in the house waiting for us. However, as his golf wins increased, my desire to be seen also increased. The media was now in our lives, and I could justify spending more and more money on my looks. In fact, I could justify nearly anything.

Today, I know I am among many women who compete with each other. As I share more of my journey toward wholeness, other women tell me they have felt the same way. There are many of us who close our hearts to each other, judging ourselves harshly and hiding our true selves. I look back on it all and wish I could have talked about these issues, sharing my fears and breaking open the polite silence that was killing me and, ultimately, my marriage. There were and are many wonderful wives and girlfriends on the tour. I believe we could have had stimulating conversations about these issues I was facing. I was so torn between wanting to express myself authentically and wanting to be seen and known as someone special. If I had talked with the other women about this, I know now I wouldn't have felt alone.

What does it take to begin a deep and courageous conversation about these topics? For me, sadly, it took a crisis. First, we have to go to the Ryder Cup.

Ryder Cup 2004

THE MASTERS TOURNAMENT IS MAGNIFICENT WORLD-CLASS golf. Qualifying to play in the Ryder Cup was his equivalent to winning a major lottery in America. I had heard of the Ryder Cup but did not know it was played every two years between teams from Europe and America. He loved telling me the history and making sure I knew that, through 1977, the teams were from Great Britain, Ireland, and the United States. It wasn't until 1979 that players from continental Europe became eligible for selection.

He said every tournament was a stepping-stone to being selected for Team Europe. He was counting on the selection team to notice that he had been the first golfer in the United States to win three consecutive PAC-10 championships. He also won the English Amateur in 1999 and 2000. In 1999, he won the Walker Cup as a member of the Great Britain and Ireland team. His big dream was to qualify for membership in both the European and U.S. tours. This happened.

I was with him the day Bernhard Langer, a legend in golf and that year's team captain, called to welcome him officially to Team Europe, Ryder Cup 2004. He wasn't surprised, as he knew his points had been mounting since September 2003, and were high enough for him to be selected. As he talked on the phone to Bernhard, I watched his face. His eyes lit up. When he hung up, he yelled, "Ryder Cup is official!" We squeezed each other, and he assured me that I was going to have the time of my life.

In those moments, everything seemed right in his world. He was experiencing the payoff for all his hard work, all the focused attention he had given to practice. Now he had the honor of participating in an event with seventy-year-old tradition.

My heart warmed when, after hugging me, he called his parents. He knew they had laid the foundation for this moment; their energy and relentless love had helped him achieve his life's dream. His parents were over-the-moon proud of him. Part of their excitement was their son telling them they would be honored guests and taken care of by the European Tour Ryder Cup committee. They deserved it.

He also acknowledged how much I had contributed to his success. He wanted to make sure I knew I was a vital part of his team and I was important to him. As you might imagine, these words meant more to me than having a great time at the Ryder Cup. I felt valued in his life.

I wondered if this might be the time he would ask me to marry him. That would have been *my* Ryder Cup. I believed that if we were married, I wouldn't need to worry anymore about another woman being by his side. I did believe marriage was forever. I was secretly convinced that he had purchased an engagement ring, and that by the time we arrived at the Ryder Cup, we would be publicly announcing our upcoming wedding. I was in a constant state of nervous expectation, hoping he would finally propose to me. I wanted my ring.

The 2004 Ryder Cup, the 35th Match, was held September 17–19 at the South Course of Oakland Hills Country Club in Bloomfield Township, Michigan, a suburb northwest of Detroit. I remember wishing it were a more exotic place, but it couldn't have been more perfect for the two of us and all of the golfers.

He had known his own points were high enough to qualify for the team. What he and others didn't know was who would get the two wild cards. They usually went to veterans or to a guy who just missed making the team by a sliver of a point. The captain chose. Colin Montgomerie and Sergio Garcia had performed so well that it was not a surprise when Bernhard made them the wild card picks. He was elated for them.

There wasn't a golfer, wife, girlfriend, coach, or caddy who wasn't thinking about it. However, we didn't talk about it much. After a while, the words "Ryder Cup" or "qualification" became mundane. The talk was about Team Europe winning!

I wanted everyone to make it, but I was especially happy when Padraig Harrington was selected. It meant Caroline would be there. I knew this would be a major media event, and she would help me figure out everything I needed to have and do. In many ways, Caroline was a mentor for me. I remember thinking that one day I hoped to pay her mentorship forward to another woman entering the golf world.

Each of the wives and girlfriends was given a large sum of money by the tour to purchase the right clothes, shoes, and jewelry for every aspect of the event. We were told the media would be following us the entire time. This meant we needed a special outfit for every event, from the moment we arrived at the airport through the following two days. We chose outfits for travel, eating breakfast, walking the course, and attending formal parties.

I was given a list of the activities and made an appointment with a personal shopper at the exclusive and luxurious department store Harrods in London. In my wildest dreams, I would never have guessed I would purchase a gown for three thousand pounds. That was over five thousand American dollars at the time!

In the gorgeous, green, leather-lined Harrods fitting room, I was introduced to the perfection of the Prada gown. Once it was zipped up, I gazed in the mirror for several minutes. I imagined him standing next to me, announcing I was the one he had chosen to be his wife. The gown was perfect. In those moments, in that gown, I was a professional golfer's fiancée at the Ryder Cup.

I heard the whisper of all the women before me. "Just buy it." But the most extraordinary saddle I wanted did not cost nearly this much. "Just buy it. The gown is fit for a queen." In that moment, I became a queen. I, a woman who had only heard of Prada, bought a gown meant for royalty, and the tour paid for it.

Once the women were together at the event, we discussed what we would wear. Suddenly, one of the golf wives brought out her jewels and invited each woman to borrow whatever she wanted. As she laid them out, all I could think about was how kind she was to share with us. I borrowed one of her gorgeous diamond bracelets. I joked that I had a perfectly good show jumper on my wrist! In that moment, my love of horses was far away. I was mesmerized by the dazzling beauty that money could buy.

One of the greatest parts of the 2004 Ryder Cup for me, besides being so happy for him, was getting to know the other women. We were all thrust together, and we became a team in our own way. We were excited, anxious, scared, energized, exhausted, and most of all, supportive of each other. Finally, I didn't feel any competition with these women. The torture of comparison faded away. I still wanted to be perfect for him, but

I felt that no matter what happened, I was backed up by these women. We were excited for each other to be the best we could be. It was one of the greatest feelings in my life. The door to genuine friendships with women, including expressing vulnerability, opened that September.

It was a little difficult being an American and cheering for the Europeans. I respected both sides and dodged every question from the media that would make it seem otherwise.

Sunday was all singles matches and considered the most nerve-wracking day of the Ryder Cup. The guys were on their own, without partners to bounce off of. On Saturday night, the captains of both teams announced their lineups. We learned who would go out first, second and so on. There were twelve tee times since there were twelve players per team. One never knew whom they were going to play until each list had been handed out.

That night, he requested to go first. He assumed the US team would put Tiger Woods, then the world's number-one ranked golfer and scariest opponent one could play, out first to set the stage and get a point on the board early. The US team was down by a few points after the previous day's play.

He assumed right. We were sitting together at a table when we learned he would be playing Tiger. I was instantly filled with butterflies and looked over at him to gauge how he felt. Initially he looked calm. Then a little smile crawled across his face. He loved competition—the more intense, the better.

I couldn't sleep that night. I couldn't stop thinking about all that was happening. I felt a combination of excitement and worry. As I lay in the hotel bed, I looked at the boxes of gifts we had been given, including exquisite crystal vases. I couldn't help but wonder when a little box with an engagement ring was going to show up.

I tried to forget about it and instead focus on my gold necklace with a miniature engraved Ryder Cup trophy. I was grateful to be a part of this historical event. I was grateful to feel so comfortable with the women and to be with him. I was scared to death for him to play Tiger.

He slept soundly. He had an incredible ability to shut down his mind. I admired that about him. I couldn't sleep. I wanted him to win. I wanted him to be happy.

He woke up wearing his game face. I always knew when he was singularly focused and ready to win. He said good morning and got ready. I had everything laid out for both of us. It was a big day. He didn't speak much at breakfast, but Sergio Garcia, the flamboyant wild-card Spaniard, made breakfast entertaining with his jokes and funny personality.

I, on the other hand, was too nervous to eat. At the entrance of the clubhouse, I looked over at Tiger's wife Elin and noticed how calm and poised she looked. I wanted to introduce myself to her, but I was convinced I would stumble over my words. She was beautiful then and still is today, inside and out.

After breakfast, I walked out to the first tee, where the crowds were swarming around the grandstands, trying to spot Tiger and him. My hands were ice cold and my throat felt like it was full of golf balls. I hoped no one noticed that I was trembling. It was the biggest day of his career in golf and everyone knew it, especially me.

Fortunately, Pernilla Bjorn, the wife of the assistant captain Thomas Bjorn, came over to support and walk with me. I was so happy to see her, I cried. She handed me a cup of hot chamomile tea. We sipped as we walked the course. This was the beginning of a friendship with Pernilla that continues to this day. She knew I needed support and knew exactly how to help me. What a wonderful gesture. It was love in action, and I'll never forget it.

It was after eight o'clock when the announcer introduced the first flight of the day. The crowd went wild. They must have been in heaven watching these two accomplished men battle it out for their nations. I secretly prayed for him to hit in the middle and for Tiger to hit way out of bounds. However, they both hit great shots, and it wasn't long until my nerve wall was cracked. I could breathe easily again.

Elin was following Tiger; we were on opposite sides of the fairway. It was hard to miss her with her long blonde hair. We met at the third hole in the back of the green. In her sweet Swedish accent, she said, "You know, we can walk together if you like."

Michael Jordan was standing next to us with a cigar the size of my arm. He shook my hand, smiled, and gestured. "Shall we, ladies?" he said, suggesting we move on to the next hole with our men.

Walking with Michael and Elin felt very comfortable. I can't explain it. Perhaps it was because they were so comfortable. Elin, in a very relaxed, casual manner, engaged me in a conversation about my horses while continuing to keep her eye on Tiger. She was so kind to me and didn't seem to worry about who was going to win or lose. I admired that. I was also appreciative that Michael Jordan didn't blow any smoke in my face!

He lost the match to Tiger. Instead of expressing disappointment, he immediately moved on to support the other players on the course. He was a true sportsman. It was clear we were *all* a team.

Somehow, he always knew where I was on the course and made it a point to connect with me. I loved that. Even when I was sipping tea or walking with Elin and Michael, my eyes were always on him. I watched the way he snapped his fingers when he wanted a ball to "sit" on the green. My heart connected to his when his name was announced on the tee and he tipped his hat as the crowd cheered. I watched his eyes when he stared a good shot down. I knew the good shots from the bad just from his body language. When our eyes locked, he always smiled the smile that was "ours." Other times he gave me a little wave with the hand hanging by his side, to let me know we were connected. If I went to the bathroom or to get a snack, he would later say, "Where were you on the fourteenth hole?"

Every time he reinforced caring for me, I thought about the ring. I hate admitting this. But if he cared so much, why weren't we engaged? At the time, making him happy was still my priority and main job. Little did I know my job would eventually become unattractive to him. Further down the road, it also became unattractive to me.

I felt like royalty carrying around a radio that broadcast the results of the other matches happening in every corner of the course. Everyone on the team was given a radio along with the option of riding in the special blue-and-yellow golf carts. In the cart, I felt like I was in a chariot pulled by two white stallions. I felt important. I felt respected.

I did have one tiff on the course with another wife. It happened at the seventeenth hole, a par three gallery with thousands of fans. He was playing with David Howell in the Saturday fourball against Jim Furyk and Chad Campbell. At the back of the green, the grandstand was packed with a sea of fans wearing red, white, and blue. The energy around this hole was electric. With two holes to play, the US team was up one—that is, unless he or David could perform a miracle. That is exactly what they did.

As we approached the green, one of the US team wives encouraged the crowd to scream louder. She was actively trying to get the noise level higher. I strutted over to her in one of my great outfits and said, "Really, do you think that is necessary? You already have thousands of people cheering for the United States." I was so mad at her.

My anger was quelled when I learned they had a chance to win, but I felt awful for getting so mad. I prayed no one had heard me and the media wouldn't find out. They would have *loved* to make a story out of my anger. When players get angry, the media is all over it. I could only imagine the stories that could have been told about a pro's raging girlfriend. He would have been furious.

I wasn't quite sure what to do, but as we walked down the fairway to the eighteenth hole, the other woman walked by me and said, "Are we okay?"

I looked at her, relieved, and said, "Yep, we are good."

I was so grateful she came up to me, because I don't think I could have apologized. As you might have gathered, I was not used to confrontation nor apologizing. I promised myself on that day that if the roles were ever reversed, I would find the courage to go up to another woman and offer kind reassurance.

The European team won the competition by a margin of 18.5 to 9.5 points. The victory was the largest by a European team in the history of the event, and the largest by either side since 1981. I wish everyone in the world could have felt the happiness we felt that day. We celebrated in our team room, which our crew (the Ryder Cup Committee) had decorated with streamers, balloons, and tons of confetti. We stayed up all night, recapping the highlights and watching the incredible motivational movie that Bernhard had created. The clips of the players winning and making extraordinary shots over the last year inspired all of us. There wasn't a person in the room with a dry eye. We all had goose bumps the size of pearls on our skin.

In addition to celebrating the team's victory, I personally celebrated my breakthrough with the golf tour women. I left the event feeling confident that I was truly ready to connect with other women and widen my world. I was, however, still only his girlfriend. There was no engagement ring.

After the Ryder Cup was over, in keeping with my hope to interact with more of the women, I offered to plan and host baby or wedding showers. I don't know how many parties I hosted, but I loved getting to know more of the women through the celebrations. I also thought it would impress him. I desperately wanted that ring.

The Media's Darling

I HAD NEVER KNOWN HOW TO DEAL WITH THE MEDIA, BUT I witnessed others handle it well. The managers held the players' hands and coached them until it was second nature. However, the women weren't formally given any instructions. He was always a natural when it came to dealing with people, and I watched him closely in the press conferences. His responses were impressive, and he paused at just the right times. He was direct, charismatic, and charming. The media loved him. I did too.

I remember watching him in Abu Dhabi, where the reporters hung on every single word, sitting on the edges of their seats, waiting for him to smile. He always spoke to the media and gave them what they wanted, even when he was exhausted or didn't want to take the time. He believed it was the responsibility of every player.

There were a few reporters who approached me while I was walking the course and asked how he was doing. Taking his lead, I interacted with them, and I shared my umbrella if it was raining. I enjoyed talking with the reporters who wanted to know more about him and about my love of horses. Eventually, I was named the Media Darling by a journalist in Ireland during the 2006 Ireland Ryder Cup. I was kind and always willing to be in a photo. I was told they liked my smile and that I appeared genuinely approachable. The reporters didn't seem to notice that I was self-conscious and fearful. I dreaded making a mistake or embarrassing him. By now, I was good at acting as if I were a professional in my own right.

As he became more successful, the unsuccessful rounds were of more interest to the media. During his peak performance years, 2006 to 2009, he was one of a handful of prospects to win more than one major. The stakes were high, so the pressure was more intense. The press came up to me during a round and asked if he was okay. I replied, "Yes, of course ... it's just one of those days. I am sure tomorrow will be a different story." The next day was reliably different because no two days are alike out on the course. Cameras were always clicking, and I was constantly calculating how I wanted to look and be perceived.

While some of the other golf wives expressed their genuine feelings and ran out on the course to congratulate their husbands, I waited at the back of the green, hoping I would appear classy and sophisticated. I could feel the fifty camera lenses pointing in my direction to get my reaction when he won. I always wore sunglasses because tears welled up with every win; my heart was so full of happiness for him. He always had a tear in his eye too, and we smiled at one another as if we had known all along he was going to win.

The media loved it when I came into the press room after a tournament to hear his post-winning speech. I loved the cameras flashing, the laptops all over the tables, even the long cords dangling along the floor. I usually sipped on a glass of champagne for the hour-long interview process.

I will never forget the first time he acknowledged me in a press conference. I was shocked. He hadn't mentioned my name for the first few wins, but in 2006 at the HSBC Match Play Championship at Wentworth, where he won one million pounds, he publicly thanked me for my support. The money and accomplishment made his day. His gratitude for me made mine.

The Crowds and Fame

THE CROWDS AT THE TOURNAMENTS COULD BE ANNOYING. It always amazed me how some people could be so supportive and loving, and others could be unmercifully cruel. He was a very popular player to watch, so the crowds were enthusiastic to see him, especially in the UK.

A few people made negative and critical comments about him, not realizing or caring that I was within earshot. I would respond with something like, "Oh and that is why *you* are on this side of the rope, right?" When they learned I was his girlfriend, they usually apologized and were embarrassed. Through the years, we learned not to take the negative comments personally; however, it was hard, and every one of us had to deal with it.

One time a spectator asked me if he ate the same food every night and if he wore boxers or briefs! I was also asked if he ever got mad and how he handled anger. They were always grateful when I politely gave them a little information that I felt was appropriate. I had to remind myself that without the fans, there would be no tournaments. We both believed the fans deserved attention.

Japan was a special place for professional golfers. The Japanese people are known for the great respect they show the players. In 2001, a young Japanese boy with a sweet, round face, dark eyes, and genuine smile gave me one of his beanie hats at the Tayheio course in Gotemba City. To thank the boy, I promised I would get him to sign some golf balls and to shake the young boy's hand. This meant the world to the boy.

I was famous for getting him to sign balls, especially for the little kids. He would always say, "J, I don't think I have that many golf balls in my bag." I met many nice people who said their greatest dream was to shake his hand and own his signed golf ball. I wanted to make their dreams come true and give them more than they could have imagined. Sometimes I was able to get them a short conversation, a handshake, a smile, *and* a signed golf ball. I loved seeing their faces light up when this happened.

Players' Lounge

MANY OF THE FEMALES ON TOUR DIDN'T CONVERSE WITH the other players. Eventually, I did. We formed some relationships with a few couples. Before or after a round, we met in the official players' lounge, a room in the clubhouse with a guard at the door and an extraordinary spread of food. Only players and families were given access. It was a great place for the players to get away from the public and media. Although golfers competed with each other, they had a lot in common and a lot to talk about. We never took vacations or socialized outside of the clubhouses, but we enjoyed many great conversations with other players and their spouses in the players' lounges.

One of my funniest memories was with Ernie Els at the Johnnie Walker Championship in Perth, Australia (2003, Lake Karrinyup Country Club). The slogan for Johnnie Walker was *Keep Walking*, and the image representing the brand was the outline of a man swiftly walking. Along the fairways, certain areas were designated as places where the spectators could cross, and 99 percent of the time these places had a sign that said "Cross here" or "Crosswalk." It was clear where to cross over the fairway in order to view the next hole without walking all the way around.

Apparently, the tournament director thought it was a good idea to put the Johnnie Walker sign with the logo and slogan at each crosswalk area. I read it as an instruction to "Keep Walking." So I did. I walked the entire length of the course, about ten miles as opposed to seven. When the round was over, I was exhausted from my very long walk. Ernie laughed hysterically as he said, "That's the slogan, not directions for the spectators." I laughed too.

I loved the discussions with players and their wives about the beautiful courses in parts of the world to which we had not yet traveled. It was fun to talk about the similarities and differences of various courses and swap information about hotels, restaurants, and walking trails.

If the public wonders whether players remain serious off the golf course, I will tell you that these guys know how to have fun. These people have big lives. There was always lots of laughter and stories to tell. I am sure there were players who didn't join in the socializing, but he loved it and was well liked. I was there because he was there. I liked being right by his side.

When we were alone, I did notice we weren't laughing as much as when we first met. I wondered if it was normal. Maybe all couples laughed less as time passed.

Mesmerized by Money

MY PARENTS WERE ROLL-UP-THEIR-SLEEVES-AND-GO-TO-work kind of people. While they recognized money was central to enjoyment in our lives, their emphasis was clearly on values and cultivating meaningful work. To this day I appreciate them for showing me the value of hard work and a fair monetary exchange. My parents and stepfather have integrity in every area of their lives, and they would all say, "Never look for money. Look for work. The money will follow."

As I mentioned earlier, I was raised in an affluent home. If there were money issues, I was never made aware of them. I was more aware that my parents wanted me and my sister to take nothing for granted and to earn our spending money. I always expected to do at least my share in every relationship.

His parents were also hard workers and understood the value of money. He often spoke about how much they sacrificed for him to play golf while he was growing up. He knew he wouldn't be a professional without their continued support.

We each knew what it was like not to have very much money, and we came to know what it was like to have a lot. When we first met and started traveling together, we had very little extra spending money. In time, this all changed.

I was surprised to learn that initially golfers must pay for their tournament accommodations and flights out of their own bank accounts. As his status improved, the tournament hosts began to pay for expensive hotels and first-class plane tickets. I had never talked with my sister about this. I had assumed players didn't have to pay for anything since so many people came to watch them. It puzzled me.

I tried to impress him by being thrifty. I spent hours researching the cheapest, nicest hotels near the tournaments. If we had to buy our own plane tickets, I learned to shop schedules and find deals. In the beginning, we longed to be in the nicer hotels. When I booked plane tickets, the most important thing to me was that we sat together. When we sat in coach, we expressed our longing for the day we would be flying first class, with the extra room and warm cashews.

I never dreamed that one day I would become so accustomed to first class that I wouldn't even notice the luxurious service. One time after boarding first class, I noticed a woman about my age staring at us in our comfortable seats. The boarding line was held up, and she stood looking at us for what seemed like a long time. She did not have the usual accessories of a woman with money. I did.

After she moved on, I wondered what she was thinking. I am sure she noticed he was holding my hand; he always held it. I was wearing AG jeans, a black Gucci custom-made blazer, and a sparkling platinum Rolex watch on my wrist. On my left hand was the O. J. Perrin ring we had picked out together during the first year he made so much money. (Here's another secret. I told him the ring he had given me didn't fit on my right hand, so I wore it on my left and pretended it was an engagement ring. I lied. That's how much I longed to be married.)

It was clear I wasn't my parents' daughter. I was taking everything for granted. We were hanging out with rich people who lived in the financial stratosphere. This was the only world I was noticing. I cringe today at how mesmerized I became once the bank account was large enough for me to purchase whatever I wanted. Deep down I knew I couldn't purchase happiness, but he could afford a diamond ring. Where was it?

We loved the lifestyle, and the more luxurious it became, the less I was missing my horses. It wasn't that I didn't love them; I was caught up in glamorous life. I do know golf professionals and spouses who do not live extravagant lifestyles—or if they do, they are not as out of touch as I became. We were often given expensive gifts, and I had become the woman who expected them. One example was a Tiffany crystal from a tour event with a card that read, "Just because." I was only mildly impressed.

I also remember the time we were invited to fly on Phil Mickelson's beautiful Gulfstream 400 private jet with "AIR PHIL" printed on the cups and napkins. By this time, while it was nice to be with him on his plane, I was so accustomed to this level of luxury that I don't think I was excited about anything.

It was an honor to be on a private plane with a man like Phil Mickelson. But because I was so mesmerized by the almighty dollar, I lost the innocent ability to feel joy and deep appreciation. I took many things for granted. When I think about this today, I feel sick inside. I was in such a dense fog of self-righteousness.

Irish Luxury

ANOTHER EXAMPLE OF MY LUXURIOUS LIFESTYLE WAS AP-parent at Adare Manor, nestled in a village in Ireland. A Irish businessman, J. P. McManus, hosted a pro-am charity event every five years where amateurs (usually celebrities and professional athletes) paid to play with professional golfers on the manor's golf course. He was asked to play, and we were very excited because we had heard it was wonderful event.

J. P. McManus was a wealthy, generous man who had made his money from horse racing. All twenty-five pro players and their wives were gifted Rolex watches, and each woman was gifted a large sum of money to spend in the village. We were shocked. We had so much fun walking as a group to the little village. We descended on one small shop where we fell in love with the real Irish cashmere sweaters, gloves, scarves, and hats. By the time we left the shop, the shelves were literally empty.

In 2009, we returned to Adare Manor in helicopters so we

could see the beautiful landscape. The first gift we received was a bag of expensive Moroccan oil products. Every man and woman received beautiful diamond watches, and the women once again were given thousands of dollars to spend in the village. This time we bought out one dress shop. It was wildly fun.

I was beginning to understand the old adage, "If you want money, be near money. Money goes where money is. You need to rub against it so that it can rub against you."

Being Managed

I WAS SURPRISED TO LEARN PROFESSIONAL GOLFERS AND their families often had management companies to assist them with tournaments and their personal needs. Gaylord Sports was his first management company. They also managed Phil Mickelson, among others. Our first house was only a ten-minute drive from the Gaylord office. This short distance made it convenient to meet with them for lunch to sign new deals.

It was Gaylord Sports that put together the deal for him to represent the energy drink Red Bull. Along with a financial retainer, we received enough cans of this high-energy drink to fill our entire garage, and a huge refrigerator just to house the cans. To represent the brand on the golf course, he carried a Red Bull metal can filled with water. I can't tell you how many times people asked me if he drank it. I was amazed so many people noticed it!

Another key role for the management company was to

negotiate club deals. Club deals are usually made between the agent and the manufacturer, such as Titleist or Nike. Prior to turning professional in November 2000, he played with Titleist. They brought a van to every US and European tournament to service all the players under contract with them. We spent many rainy days in the van, which was equipped with a lounge and a small shop where golf clubs were tweaked or fixed. The players also stopped by the van on their first day of a tournament to collect balls, hats, tees, rain gear, and gloves. I liked to spend time in the van because I enjoyed the tour representatives and seeing what happens behind the scenes. I was impressed with how everyone was focused on helping the players play their best.

As he gained more status, I encouraged him to consider signing on with the International Management Group based in Cleveland, Ohio, and London. I had met Guy Kinnings, the CEO, at a few of the tournaments and liked him. He was a British lawyer with impeccable style. I encouraged him to go with IMG because this group would help his reputation. I spent a lot of time researching this so that when I made the suggestion to him, I was armed with my facts and reasons. My mom always taught me to be with the best of the best.

However, he made the decision not to sign on with a management company. Instead, he hired an experienced marketing agent who worked with Bentley and Aston Martin, two prestigious car manufacturers in the UK. Of course, I accepted whatever he thought was best. I also took on the job of helping to shape his image. It was my job to handle all the flight and hotel bookings, as well as all the at-home duties. I had always been protective of him, but I became even more so as he gained status. After all, his status also felt like mine.

After the Ryder Cup fever, he publicly said some words about the US team that were taken *way* out of context. At that time, his focus was on the World Cup in Seville, Spain, where he would be playing with Luke Donald. I remember it all so well. It was a Tuesday morning when we woke up to his BlackBerry beeping in our beautiful hotel room in Seville. He was receiving hate mail. I became very concerned because I considered it my job to keep him happy, especially before a tournament. There were 683 messages on his phone, mostly comments suggesting he never step back into the United States. We both felt terrible about what had happened. I am not sharing more because that is his story. I can tell you that all of it was very unsettling. I was shocked at how much the media distorted his words.

Wanting to help, I told him my parents had taught me to smile, be kind, and give them something else to talk about. That is exactly what he did. He played better than ever, making some thirty-foot putts and laser 4 irons. He and Luke won the World Cup. When they lifted up the Wedgewood trophy together, the public anger faded into the sunset.

Perks

SPECIAL PERKS FOR THE PLAYERS AND WIVES WERE DEPEN-
dent on status. As he became more famous as a top athlete, more
doors started to open. When he signed with IMG (International
Management Group) in 2005, our world changed. They were and
are the best of the best, the ultimate in sports management. Soon
after signing, we expressed an interest in attending Wimbledon.
We called our manager, Guy, and he was on it like white on rice.
Two days after making the request, we were sitting with Roger
Federer's wife in the Wimbledon players' lounge. It was incredible. Even though it rained that day and they didn't get to play,
the fact that we were able to get tickets was more than we had
ever imagined. I loved the indulgence, the comfort, the riches,
and the entire lifestyle.

Sadly, just receiving those tickets made me feel like a very big
deal. The feeling of being special was not sustaining. The feeling

of being above others created an incredible but false rush. I didn't recognize what the rush was doing to me.

Before he became an ambassador for Rolex in 2007, we received steep discounts on any timepieces. Once he signed on, we were treated like part of a Rolex royal family. BMW was gracious in giving us cars to use while we were in the UK and United States. We could each choose whatever BMW we wanted. He usually wanted something with a big engine.

Prior to the tour, I had not paid attention to cars. I grew to love, love, love fancy cars. Though I had been raised in an upper financial bracket, my parents' lifestyle was certainly not like the one we were now living. We were living the American Dream, and it catapulted us into another world. On the surface I enjoyed the decadence, but underneath I knew something was out of sync. Deep inside, I knew there was more to life than fancy cars and lots of money. There had to be.

With the exception of at the Ryder Cups and in Ireland, wives were never gifted jewelry. Each year he participated in a Ryder Cup, a new captain was appointed, and this meant there was a new ladies' captain. Upon arrival, we would always find two beautifully wrapped boxes in our room. Several times we received a Rolex watch from the captain. In the other box would be a gift from the captain's wife. One year we received a necklace with a Ryder Cup emblem surrounded by diamonds. The ladies' captain was responsible for designing the jewelry piece for the women, so every year the piece was completely different. I had so much jewelry by now that the only real excitement was seeing the new design. I was always amazed by the ladies' captain's creativity.

Vacations

THE GOLF SEASON WAS PACKED FROM BEGINNING TO END due to the fact the European Tour played a full schedule. The PGA Tour, however, had a break around September, and I always felt jealous that my American friends got to be home for so long. In the beginning I didn't think much of it because being on tour was fun, but when I became more attached to my horses, it was harder to stay away for so many months. He played a season from the second week of January to the third week of December, so there was very little time off.

I convinced him one year that we should start taking vacations. For the first five years we had not taken *one* vacation. Not a single holiday was spent away from golf. Our first trip was to Jackson Hole, Wyoming, for a ski holiday.

I was most interested in making sure he enjoyed himself. We decided to take our two best friends and booked rooms at the Four Seasons hotel. Most of our time was spent laughing hysterically at just about anything. We went dog sledding, and for my birthday we went on a carriage ride. Snowmobiling was the highlight of that particular trip. The boys had a bet that the women would tip over first, and they were right. I remember having so much fun being away from the golf world. There was life outside of golf, and I loved it.

We also began to take trips in the summer, but those were different for some reason. It felt like we were always in the middle of the season, and he missed out on golf activities. We went to Italy with a friend who had a boat on Lake Garda, a beautiful town outside of Venice. We visited Venice in July 2007 for a couple of days and stayed at the fabulous Cipriani Hotel, which had the only pool on the island of Venice.

I noticed that we had nothing to talk about if we were by ourselves. It was awkward. I couldn't help but think maybe we were beginning to fall apart. We couldn't talk about anything but golf, managers, or deals. We picked out a whippet puppy, Popcorn, which gave us something to talk about while we sat at the harbor and ate dinner. I longed for meaningful conversations with him, but had no clue what that meant. It was as if neither of us knew how to relax with one another, which was strange because by this point we had been together for well over seven years.

We had the most fun together when we invited other couples to be with us or had some sort of distraction. It was becoming increasingly difficult to be with each other. Maybe that was one of the reasons for the next distraction.

Finally ... Marriage

WITH ALL MY HEART I BELIEVED A WEDDING RING WOULD erase my concerns about losing him, and I could finally stop trying to prove my worth. He was a man of integrity; marriage would be forever. At that time I didn't know how quickly forever can be deleted.

He chose to propose to me the afternoon of December 19, 2007. I am not going to share the details of the proposal. It's mine to remember, but I will tell you that it was tender and romantic and sincere. I hope you have had many tender moments in your life and can simply remember the moments. They are precious and for me, and private.

We set the marriage date for Sunday, December 14, 2008, in Scottsdale, Arizona.

I planned the wedding with a sense of urgency. At some level, I was afraid he would change his mind or something would inter-fere. I wanted to get everything arranged immediately. He must have felt like he couldn't stop this train even if he wanted to. I completely bypassed his request to slow it all down.

For the next year, my time was 100 percent focused on the wedding, traveling with him on the tour, and riding horses—that is, with the exception of when our kitchen caught fire five weeks before the wedding. We were in Spain at the Volvo Masters, watching the show *CSI* in our hotel room, when I happened to check my little Nokia phone. One of the messages was from our realtor, stating that our house was on fire. Apparently, the toaster was left plugged in when we went to Spain. It short-circuited, and the fire seriously damaged our home. It was a real shock and a big deal to both of us. However, because he was playing in the tournament, I headed back alone the next day. I was thankful the insurance company covered most everything. Things were fairly quickly put back together. It was indeed a distraction from the wedding planning, which maybe I needed a break from. He handled his emotions in his usual calm manner but was most concerned about the Jura coffeemaker he had purchased in Switzerland! Fortunately it was okay.

I hired a wedding planner to help me organize everything. She knew I was a designer, and she also knew I wanted everything a particular way. I was kind in explaining what I wanted, but I was direct and absolute. He and I agreed the ceremony and the reception should be held in the same location. We wanted it to be comfortable for our guests. Neither of us was religious, so a church was not necessary.

My colors were crème and navy blue—royal colors. My three bridesmaids looked stunning in floor-length navy-blue gowns. I wore a silver ice-blue custom designed gown, handmade by Ramona Kaveza. My hairdresser and makeup artists came to our home the day of the wedding to prepare us.

My veil was beautiful. I was surprised how much I loved it. I had been worried it might look too traditional with my modern dress. It didn't. It was perfect, and I knew he was going to love it. After the ceremony we immediately went out to finish the photography. I took the veil off and left it in our dressing room. When I went back later, it was gone and never to be found. Everyone thought it had been stolen. I was surprised that I wasn't upset. I felt such love surrounding me. I thought, "I hope whoever has it enjoys it." Inside the rim of the veil was a label with my maiden name, Hefner. I wasn't Hefner anymore. I was married and loved taking his last name.

Our wedding vows were written with the man who served as our ceremony officiate, Dr. Don Greene, whom we both worked with on mindfulness and sports performance. Our vows were sweet and kind, but I don't know if I was emotionally present when we were expressing the words. I was more interested in the decor, every inch of it. Our wedding was a beautiful performance. I wanted it to *look* perfect.

It was raining buckets on our day. I had to respond quickly, so I chose to have a $6,000 extralarge tent constructed. I ordered the setup team to get right at it and didn't tell him about the money I was spending. I also didn't keep track of expenditures— a reminder of how out of touch I was with the everyday world. Every single person we invited attended. Every one. One hundred and sixty people. Needless to say, this was an expensive wedding. I didn't care. I thought our money was endless.

It seemed like a million photos were taken, and I believe I was only truly present in one photograph. We were standing on the patio, looking out at Camelback Mountain after the rain stopped and as the sun was setting. The photographer asked if he would hold his hands around my face. I always wanted him to do this but was too afraid to ask him. I was afraid he would think it was corny. Following directions from the photographer, he quickly rubbed his hands together to warm them up. When he held my face, tears rolled down my cheeks. In that moment, I felt overwhelming love for him.

When we were introduced as husband and wife in the reception room I had designed, I felt like a queen, and he was the king. I had decided to give the welcome speech. He didn't want to speak in front of everyone even though he had made a dozen winning speeches. I was honored.

My speech was short. As I looked out at the participants, I could see how beautiful everything was. The walls were covered in thirty-feet-high sheer white silk curtains. All the tables and chairs were white. White flowers adorned every table. Special lighting had been brought in from California. It all looked perfect.

We had a little sweetheart table instead of sitting at a head table. When I saw the sign with our married names on the table, my heart suddenly filled with doubt. My insecure thoughts hadn't gone away. The ring was on my finger, and yet I was afraid. The inner whisper that I was not enough and another woman would take him away was louder than ever. I was shocked.

Each of the reception tables was named after famous horses. Our family sat at "Corso," named after our beloved Holsteiner gelding. He was an Olympic and National World Cup champion with an impressive list of wins. Corso was our best horse and the first horse he ever bought me. We wanted to honor our families with his name.

The reception was spectacular, with a band everyone thought was out of this world. He wanted to catch up with everyone he hadn't seen in a while, like Maury Povich and Connie Chung, while I danced with our guests. I took my shoes off and danced for four straight hours. I was in heaven. While dancing, my insecurities drifted. I was Mrs. Him, and I could dance and feel respected by his peers.

We paid for all of our guests to stay at the Four Seasons Hotel the night of our wedding. Our families had arrived a week before to enjoy the weather, gym, spa, and good food the hotel offered. It was wonderful to have everyone in the same place and so close to us during this special time.

After the reception ended at two in the morning, we went to our penthouse suite far away from the main lobby of the hotel. When we opened the door, we were greeted with what seemed like millions of flowers. The florist had taken the flowers from our ceremony and decorated our room. Lilies, hydrangeas, and roses were in every corner. The sweet fragrance felt like a blessing to us.

He knew my feet hurt, so he drew me a bath in the deep, gorgeous white tub. As I soaked in the tub, he sat on the teak bench next to me. We recalled the night's events. We were happy and couldn't stop smiling.

I wanted my life to appear as a fairy tale. I was the princess in my ice-blue gown. He was my Prince Charming. I wanted everyone to think every single detail of the wedding was perfect. I was perfect. He was perfect. We were perfect.

The next morning I had arranged for a brunch to be held for both of our families. We joined together for a little food and exchanged stories from the night before.

Honeymoon

OUR HONEYMOON WAS AS PERFECT AS OUR WEDDING: EX-
actingly planned and executed like clockwork. The day after our
wedding, we headed out for the Chevron World Challenge at the
Sherwood Country Club in California. It was our favorite tournament of the year, mainly because we could bring Coolwhip, our
beloved whippet, and stay at the Four Seasons Hotel. The tournament director was helpful and tried to make the event feel like a
honeymoon. It did. Again, the details are private. But underneath
the current of fear that was still inside me, I was happy. Our first
year together was filled with laughter, dreams, and romance.

Part II: The Years of Change

Changes

In late 2008, the year we married, he told me that he wanted to move to Paradise Valley, a small area in Scottsdale where all the houses had at least one acre of land. I wasn't attracted to the area. You rarely saw nature or had rainy days. We had been living to the north, fifteen miles away, and I loved it there. Lying in our bed, we could see gorgeous Pinnacle Peak in the distance, and I could smell nature all around me. I loved the silence and the view; it was wide and vast. When I walked into our four-thousand-square-foot modern house with more windows than I could count, I always felt I was at home. I loved everything about it. It was not small but by no means as large as the houses in Paradise Valley. We had made trips to Paradise Valley many times, since his coach, Peter Kostis, lived there. Every single time, I couldn't wait to get back to our neighborhood.

I felt guilty for not liking Paradise Valley. Nevertheless, I voiced my opinion of not wanting to live there. But he loved it, and of course, I wanted his happiness more than my own. At this point he was traveling more to Asia and the Middle East to design golf courses. It made sense to live closer to the airport. I had a feeling he was going to make a good case for a move. He did.

One Sunday morning while I was reading *Horse & Rider* on the patio and sipping my coffee, he came out to show me a house he had found in the neighborhood where he wanted to live. I immediately bristled, but he persuaded me to look. It was on the outskirts of Paradise Valley, which made me feel better, and it wasn't next to a big, sprawling mansion. Eventually I said yes.

It wasn't long until we were standing in front of our new home, designed by Ned Sawyer, a student of Frank Lloyd Wright. He had so much respect for the design of the house; he always admired people who were talented. We named the house Fanfol (it was on Fanfol Drive) and dreamed about all the changes we wanted to make it not only ours, but fantastically ours.

I resisted making drastic changes until one day I noticed how happy and alive he became when he was on site, watching the tennis court being ripped up by construction workers. We made trips together to the site every other day, but I was on site every single day. As you might imagine, I wanted to run the show. My control and perfectionism were at their peak. I made sure that whenever he was coming to see the changes, everything was managed. I was very protective and not about to let anyone make my husband upset. I didn't want to risk his golf game being compromised. We spent most of our off-season time with another architect, Rich Fairborn, who is someone I adore to this day.

As we restored the main house and added a four-thousand-square-foot extension, we wanted to keep the budget below $750,000. By the end, we would spend over $2 million *just* on the renovation. I was completely caught up in having the perfect everything for my perfect husband. I chose over-the-top appliances and furniture. With these choices came a desire for every inch of the house to be immaculate, a showpiece. When we moved into Fanfol in 2010, a crew came three times a week to clean, among everything else, our favorite room in the house—the marble bathroom. I decreased my time at the barn so I could manage the staff.

If you had seen me then, you would have seen a robot-like woman who was constantly cleaning, vacuuming, ordering the crews around, and fixing anything out of order or even slightly out of place. The house was an immaculate masterpiece by the time we were done. It was very livable, if only we had known how to live. I had become increasingly cold, rigid, and emotionally distant. I rarely noticed him. I only appreciated him if he was putting everything in its proper place. The house was cold on the hottest of days. It felt like a freezer locker—frosty.

I know today that my desire for control was out of control. I didn't know it then, but I realized something wasn't right with me.

The "something not right" was complicated. Outside of the house, it looked like everything was more than right. We looked like we lived the good life. The whisper of fear in me was supposed to have gone away, but it hadn't. Each time I felt I wasn't enough, I desperately tried to control everything. Some days I cleaned more than other days, but every day I cleaned and organized something.

As my attention to details in the outer world increased, the distance between him and me increased. I didn't think about it. I thought if I kept everything clean, everything would be okay. The towels were perfectly stacked. His socks were whiter than white. The kitchen counters were perfectly clear. Everything was going to be okay. I knew he loved everything clean and organized as much as I did. In fact, I think he liked it more than me. We were a good match. However, there was a whole lot behind my need to have everything perfect.

Eventually, we were like two passing ships. We rarely spoke to one another and never discussed our distance. We crawled into the same bed without looking at or touching each other. I don't think either of us wanted to see what was happening. He had a big life full of his exercise routine, working with his coaches, and tournaments. I was supervising the cleaning crew and finding respite in the barn with my horses. That is, until one day when the fog lifted.

Just as I didn't know why he chose December 19 to propose to me, I didn't know why the fog started to lift. I could no longer feel his spirit in the living room, the kitchen, or the bedroom. He was disappearing. We were disappearing. He was home less and less. When we did communicate, I was very short with him, and he was more and more impatient with me. There were times when we were around other people at tournaments and events, but we each rowed our own boat.

Then one morning, I did what many people do. I said that I thought we needed to see a therapist. I honestly can't tell you why I blurted this out. It wasn't a premeditated thought. I simply thought it and said it.

Seeking Therapy

It wasn't easy for either of us to admit that we needed professional help with our relationship. As soon as I did, our distance became even more apparent. I was terrified. My mind was spinning. Stepping into the truth of my own heart felt like a burning fire under my tired feet. A close friend suggested I go see a husband-and-wife therapist team with whom she had once found help and comfort. Quick fixes were not new to me, so it was natural to call and get an appointment immediately. For most of my life, I had felt responsible for fixing everyone and everything.

I longed to understand why I felt so disconnected from him and from life. He was at a tournament at the time of the appointment, so I went there alone. During the three-hour session, I cried and cried for the first time in many years. I softened and somehow removed my protective armor. In between wiping my tears, I shared everything I thought was wrong with me. I was honest. I did think I was defective, but I blamed him in part for our distance. My ego did not want to let him get away with being perfect while I sat in a puddle, shaming myself.

They insisted we come back together to get clear on how we would proceed and how they would be able to help us. Knowing this would be hard, I waited until he came home from his event to discuss our going. By now, I was a master at determining when to talk with him.

It took a little bit of persuading, but he agreed to see the therapists with me. I did not share that each three-hour session cost $900 because I knew the cost would make him mad. The morning prior to our session, I anticipated what it might be like. I filled the check out and folded it, hoping he wouldn't see it as I passed it to the couple when we arrived. I also knew I would cry, so I brought some cough drops to distract myself. I tried to wear clothes that didn't reveal my ultrathin frame. I didn't want them to ask if I had an eating disorder. I didn't—I had a disease of the heart. It was breaking, and I had no glue.

We sat next to one another, but it was strange. I couldn't feel him sitting next to me. Everything in the room felt cold, especially him. The therapist looked at him and dove right in: "On a scale from one to ten, how much do you love Jocelyn today?"

I looked at him and hoped he would at least say eight. He said "Seven." I hated this rating game. When asked the same question, I said, "Eleven."

The next question was, "How much do you want your marriage to Jocelyn to work?"

He said, "Nine." Finally, I felt some relief. Of course he wanted to make it work. It didn't occur to me to even think he might not. My answer again was "Eleven."

After talking about our distance, the therapists suggested we spend more time with each other. We were encouraged to cook together, walk the dogs, and learn to use our camera. He was willing to follow their instructions, but it was obvious that he hated it. After a couple of more sessions, we decided they probably weren't the right therapists for us. We weren't sure what we needed, but we knew it wasn't someone suggesting we do activities together.

The truth was, I didn't enjoy doing anything with him at that point. The saying "There's an elephant in the room" was so true. Neither of us was going to work around an elephant that we could feel. It didn't have a name or location, and we didn't know its size or impact. It felt absurd to spend time together doing anything other than trying to get to the truth of what was causing our distance.

I felt like rotting fruit that had dropped from a tree. One night, wanting to escape from the emotional distance, I decided to watch the movie *Eat Pray Love.* I cried the entire time. I fell to my knees and remembered that a close friend had given me the name of a woman, Moe, from whom she had received help. I called Moe to see if I could get an appointment for an intensive session. I booked a two-day residential weekend for December 15. I didn't know what else to do.

A Message to the Reader

AT THIS POINT, YOU WILL BEGIN TO LEARN MORE ABOUT MY internal struggles and gradual awakening process. While it has helped me to share these struggles, please remember that I am sharing this journey for the benefit of anyone who might find in my despair some way out of their own.

I am also sharing this in hopes that you too will share your stories. I want all of us to tell our stories and what we have learned in the various stages of our lives.

The distance between my heart and mind was unexplored territory, despite all the books I had read. My longing for inner peace had always been directed outward toward people, places, or things. At this point in my journey, I hadn't found inner peace in exotic places or with extravagant things. I hadn't found it with him. My heart felt like stone.

While initially resistant, eventually I began a serious and sincere journey to heal. I met wonderful people and was offered brief glimpses of a divine connection, but my rational mind told me none of it was real. I wanted proof. I didn't know that I needed my own experience and relationship with my higher power, without an intermediary.

Today, I have moved closer to inner peace through prayer, meditation, sitting in silence, and studying sacred principles that remind me to be "in the world but not of it." Before it could be this natural for me, however, I wandered around a lot. I ventured out of my comfort zone to see how others had found their way. Eventually the stone in my heart dissolved as many open-hearted people modeled compassion and shared their stories.

I know my journey doesn't offer any new messages. In fact, my path has been rather simplistic compared to those of many of the people I have met. Yet if the ultimate goal of all religions and spiritualities is union with our divine source, there must be as many different ways to meet there as there are fingerprints.

Before I tell you about meeting Moe, I want you to know a little about her. What I have to share about her was revealed over a period of years. I had to convince her that I wanted to know more about her. Initially, she didn't share much about her own journey because she was completely focused on mine. However, I knew her life story must have been filled with moments when she also felt lost. I knew because, without words, I could feel her compassion and her unwavering desire for me to wake up and simply, as she put it, grow up. Through our entire journey together, Moe was relentless about preventing any dependency on her. She insisted that I always go within and find my own voice, my own truth. She encouraged me to sit with many different people and explore many different paths.

At times, being with her was shocking. When I asked her for feedback, her responses were often a radical departure from what I had learned in my own life. I will never forget a time I was setting the table for dinner. I put the knife and the spoon on the right, the fork on the left—the "right" way. She smiled. I asked her what she was smiling about. She shared that as a young girl, she had also learned that was the proper way to set a table. However, in her growing-up process, she began to see that this form was just one of many "societal collective agreements." If she wanted to be proper according to this agreement, she needed to place the utensils exactly as I was doing.

I took a long pause after she said this and remembered that each time she prepared the table, everything was different. Sometimes, for example, the spoons might be in an empty glass. Yet it was very clear that she consciously respected the collective agreement. Each time I came to see her, I was given one wooden bowl for all our meals. I was responsible for cleaning and using that one bowl. Sometimes she offered me a sweet potato for breakfast!

I wondered about her journey. In time, the following is what I learned.

Moe was raised in a highly accomplished, academically oriented family. She was the youngest of three children and the most rebellious. Her parents attended the Unitarian church. While she loved exploring world religions along with her girlfriends, she often joked about those who actually believed there was a God. She wanted proof for everything. She was so irreverent that she would sing, "Bebop a' Jesus, he's my savior" and "Father, Son, and Holy Ghost, whose the one you love the most?" while hysterically laughing about the born-again Christians in her neighborhood.

Then migraine headaches took over her life. In the late 1950s, when she was in her early teens, the family doctor, in his white lab coat and round spectacles, stated the likelihood she would have migraines all her life because they were in her family history. His words became imprinted on her brain. She interpreted them to mean her body wasn't healthy. She felt mortified that she might have to live the rest of her life with nausea and a solid ball of fire just above the eyes.

She started taking Excedrin at four thirty in the morning to dull the pain of the migraine before she started her day. She continued to take Excedrin throughout the day to push through the heat of the cerebral pain. Eventually she became emotionally and physically dependent on the vascular constrictors. She didn't tell many people about the migraines because, like me, she was ashamed to show any weakness.

When she shared, "Jocelyn, I wasn't following my own grain in life, and my migraines were calling me to the life I was meant to live," I gasped. We laughed hard when she said that her first husband was and remains a wonderful man, but being a teacher of zoology, he loved snakes. At one time she allowed him to keep snakes in their on-campus apartment because she wanted to please him, but eventually she became scared to death of the snakes. She didn't want to hurt his feelings, and she also didn't want to be caught in a lie—initially she had said she liked all the snakes in the apartment. She had mastered not expressing any feelings that might cause disharmony.

But the pressure of the migraines became so intense that the twenty-three Excedrin a day and trips to the ER to get shots of Demerol stopped working. She held a prestigious position at a top university, and yet she felt she was dying.

Following is an excerpt from one of Moe's personal writings about her life:

> In my late twenties I woke up around four in the morning with the familiar headache throb. My first thoughts were directed to assessing how much pain had taken hold. Sometimes I could

feel the pain train coming down the cerebral tracks, other times it was already there. I would quietly make my way to the bathroom floor where I wrapped my body in a deep amber colored cotton blanket as I waited for the first early morning dose of Excedrin to lessen the pain. The first dose would slightly dull the edges of the knifing pain. The second dose would penetrate the heated curse a little more than the first. Throughout the day, every hour I would take another and another.

While lying on the bathroom floor, I distracted my mind from the throbbing by inviting images from around the world to surface in my consciousness --- I imagined a neighborhood in Southern China, herds of giraffes running across the African tundra, small villages of people bowing to the early morning or evening mist, doorways in Columbia, highways in Japan, thatched roofs in Ireland, the smiling face of a bride, little children in plaid shirts playing kickball, elders sitting in nursing homes eating their breakfast, and junkyards full of rusted out cars. I saw the skyscrapers in New York City, pine forests in the Rocky Mountains, and small cafes in southern France. I traveled the world and as various scenes entered the screen of my mind, I blessed each and every one.

Despite the migraine, I was grateful I could lie on my bathroom floor, wrapped in my blanket, and mentally travel the world. I knew the early morning sun would make her way and send her rays of light through the small window by the sink. However, at some level I didn't believe I would have migraines for the rest of my life. I didn't know how or when they were going to end, but I trusted that somehow the pain would derail. I had to trust this. I also knew that despite my pain, I wasn't the only one in the early morning hours in pain. I knew many people were suffering all around the world. Many of us must do hard. I knew someone, somewhere in the world was caught in the cerebral pain train with me.

The idea that others also suffered helped me to feel less alone because I had learned not to tell anyone about my migraines. If I did slip and mention it, I was flooded with all sorts of advice and repeatedly told I needed to learn to relax and not take life so seriously. Admittedly, I was driven and ambitious to excel in all aspects of life. I longed to be around people who were like me. I looked for them everywhere. Whenever I met people who were more like me (my tribe) my life at home seemed smaller and smaller. Sitting across the kitchen table with my husband, I could feel the tightness of our conversations. He would put limits on life while I was taking the gates down.

One day I decided to try to tell him about my travels to other parts of the world in the early morning as I lay on the bathroom floor. He listened, scratched his head and told me I was weird. There was no interest, no playfulness, and no curiosity. However, when I felt his judgment that day, I noticed something. I noticed how my body tightened and how stiff I felt as I tried to protect my heart from his judgment of me. I noticed that I often felt I had given him a tightrope to put around my neck so I could only go so far.

Noticing this with him, I began to also notice what happened when I began to feel self-conscious or judged by someone outside of our home. I noticed that one hundred percent of the time when I felt judged, it was as if a nuclear bomb went off in my body, and the pathways to my heart closed down. I also noticed that when I was around people who could fly with ideas and who wanted to expand their view of the world, my body relaxed, my heart and spirit opened, and my forehead was quiet.

I started to pay close attention, and realized I was mostly living around people who looked at life in terms of right and wrong, should's and should not's. I was around people who believed you had to drink three glasses of milk a day and who never considered this guideline might be being promoted by the dairy industry.

Gradually, I realized I was a trying to squeeze my consciousness into a world way too narrow for me. My energy was bigger than my container. However, I loved the people I was around. I valued them. It was confusing to want more than their kindness. Why couldn't that be enough? I only knew it wasn't. I was tired of keeping my inner travels a secret and taking Excedrin every day.

I began to see that in order to live in this constricted world, I would have to keep reaching for the Excedrin bottle and traveling the world alone in the bathroom. This awareness was breaking my heart as well as my head. I couldn't stand it anymore, but I didn't know how to expand my life with people who already felt they were expanded.

So one day, I walked backwards to my office. I waved to the neighborhood as I slowly, step by step, made my way the couple of blocks to campus. This wasn't a well-thought out plan. It just happened.

Somehow I knew I had to change my life and try to see every single thing from a different perspective. I invited others to join me in widening the view on the programs we were offering at the university; I took my lunch out of the staff lounge and ate on the manicured lawn, asked the janitor to remove all the florescent lights in my office and put in warmly lit lamps, and told my secretary to take the afternoon off and do something outrageous for a change. Gradually, I started rocking my world. With each rock, the pain train rocked and gradually ... ... derailed in favor of the expanded view.

Moe's journey from this point became a search for what she termed "the More." While she tried to appreciate the mystery in some aspects of life, she couldn't let go of her need for proof. She became curious about something more than the logical and rational mind.

In 1979, as her migraines increased, she asked for a divorce, admitting that he had done nothing wrong. She resigned from her university position to find a way to live—really live, her grain in life. With tears in her eyes, she shared that she had surrendered full custody of her precious five-year-old son to his father with the understanding that if she lived, her son could be with her at any time. Her journey included falling in love with a psychotic man and being held captive in a cabin for many months.

Row, Row, Row Your Boat

THIS IS AN EXCERPT FROM HER WRITINGS ABOUT THE CABIN that she eventually shared with me:

> When I resigned from my tenured university position and hit the road in search of God, my mother wrote me a long letter. She was rightfully very concerned that her daughter was "undoing" her life. It had appeared as if I had it all --- a great marriage, a cherished son, a beautiful home, and a prestigious university position. She was proud to tell her friends about my success in the world.
>
> Sadly, I had never been able to tell my mother the truth about my life. My marriage wasn't great; I felt stifled and alone. My husband was a scientist, and while he was a really good man, I had

dreamed of adventure in my life rather than security. Our home was beautiful, and I liked it. In fact I liked it a lot, but I don't love things. I felt I wasn't able to truly be a present, alive, Mom for my son. I was told once that the greatest gift we can give our children is to help them fall in love with life. How could I show him this when I wasn't in love with life, battling daily migraine headaches, and feeling like I was going to die? My position at the university was killing me. I had to follow guidelines and regulations all day long, and I wanted a creative life where I didn't always know what was going to happen. I wanted to be with people who were interested in exploring the inner and outer worlds rather than working toward the safety net of tenure. I felt like I was always crawling out of my skin, and I was. Most of all, I wanted to heal and to fall in love with life again.

The story of my resignation and leaving "home" is a story unto itself. This is the story about what happened once I stepped out of the secure life of a predictable marriage and career. Admittedly, I am not going to take you all the way into this story, but I will give you a glimpse. I will open the window a little so you can peek in and see there's a pot of hot water boiling on the stove. I will give you just the edges of the truth.

How and where I met Dan is not important. What's important to know is that I really thought I had met the love of my life when I met him. Dan was fifteen years older than me and was a true adventurer. He had traveled the outer world with ease most of his life and had also explored the inner worlds as a student of philosophy, journalism, and ethics. In our first encounter he quoted Voltaire, and I guess you could say he won me over with his ability to integrate massive amounts of information. It seemed that no matter what he did he excelled, and in some ways, he was bigger than life to me. He wasn't like the men I had met in graduate school or the university. Dan was a dreamer, and he knew how to dream out loud and paint pictures with words and invite others to join the dream. In retrospect, Dan had charisma. He was quick, present, articulate, and seemed to be one step ahead of anyone he was around. He loved beauty and often commented on the glimmer in someone's eyes or how the lines in an older woman's face helped him know that life was to be truly lived. In some ways, Dan reminded me of my father. There were times when he would be quiet for days, as if something was brewing in him. My dad was quiet at times too.

Eventually we rented a fairly secluded cabin nestled in Juniper trees in the back section of a sizeable horse ranch. The owner was an older, widowed woman who wanted to exchange rent for help with gardens, the horses, and the land. We thought it was the perfect fit. It was only much later that I learned why the woman never ventured to see me back in the cabin, nor would she make herself available when I was in the garden or the barn. Within a few months, Dan told her I was seriously ill, and I needed to be left alone. Secretly, they had agreed that all communication would take place between the two of them. She proceeded to tell the mailman and anyone who entered "the ranch" that our cabin and the woman who lived in it were off limits.

I felt the distance from her and others and didn't know why. Gradually, what had seemed like an idyllic life, I became aware that my world was getting smaller and smaller. Personal mail for me stopped, the phone was removed (he said it wasn't working), and there was no transportation that I could use to go anywhere by myself. At first I had appreciated the slower paced life and not having to interact with so many people. However, my only interaction was with Dan, and his quiet periods were becoming longer and longer. The once fun-loving, adventurous guy I had met was fading rapidly. When I suggested that I wanted to widen my world and meet some friends and be a part of the community, the door shut, and was locked. Dan stared at me with animal-like eyes and told me that I was now his possession, and my only world would now be whatever he wanted it to be. He told me if I ever, ever, attempted to walk out of the cabin without his permission, he would kill me. I knew this was a serious and sincere threat. I also knew that he was capable. I was with a person who could switch his personality in a second.

The few times we went out in public, he was the old charming Dan to anyone who crossed our path. Then, as soon as we were alone, there was the deadly silence, the staring, and eventually the shaking.

He loved to feed the wood-burning stove on summer days, which made the cabin unbearably hot; then watch me suffer. He loved to shake my shoulders with my head throbbing back and forth, and tell me that I would not see the light of day if I ever tried to leave him. He laughed when I learned that he had taken my address book, made a flyer, and sent it to many of my friends. The flyer was so painful I can't repeat it here, but he signed my name and basically said that I was dropping out of the culture and would never see any of them again.

Me, the one who had left her glamorous university position to go find God; me the one who wanted to lead an adventurous, creative life; me the one who wanted to add more love in the world and reap the preciousness of the gifts of life, was now held captive in a cabin with a psychotic man. After he threatened me and gave me the rules to live by, I knew how sick he really was, and how sick I was to have bypassed this monstrous part of him. It was as if once he had exposed this side of himself, he was unleashed to behave however he wanted to behave. Sometimes in the middle of the night he would wake me up and make me listen to a lecture about the state of the world. I don't know if his lectures made any sense or not because by then, I had lost over twenty-five pounds, was weak, and at times, barely able to lift my head to listen. If I didn't keep my eyes open he would scratch my face, screaming, "Wake- up." Of course, he knew that no one would hear us, and he knew, absolutely, that no one knew what was going on. He had covered all his bases --- every single one.

Perhaps what he hadn't banked on was how pathetic I had become. As I surrendered and stopped fighting the shaking and the heat, it wasn't so much fun for him anymore. He had enjoyed the struggle. I wish I could tell you that surrender was a carefully thought-out strategic move to survive ... I wish I had figured this all out and surrendered long before, but I couldn't. With all my heart I wanted to live, and as long as I could fight, I did. Then finally, I couldn't fight him anymore. I don't remember ever feeling like I didn't want to live. I just didn't have the strength to reach for life.

Now that he was fairly bored with me, he decided to get a day job in town. This meant that I would be locked in the cabin from early morning until later in the day. He warned me that I would never know if he was sitting out on the road or not, since he was allowed to leave his job whenever he wanted. He also told me that he knew every inch of the cabin, and if one thing was disturbed or I opened a window, it would cost me my life.

In the hours while he was gone, there were days when all I could do was to stare out the window. I don't remember my feelings. I just knew to follow orders.

What I do remember is the day that I noticed the Juniper trees swaying outside the window and the fierce sound of the wind. If the wind had blown hard before that day, I hadn't heard it, but this day, I did. As I listened, I started to breathe again. The wind was breathing life back into me. At first my breathing was shallow, but as the wind increased, so did my breath; and for the first time in months, I started to feel alive again. In and out, deeper and deeper, my breath began to fill up my body. With each breath, I felt my lungs expanding, and I started to quietly sing one of my favorite childhoods songs, "Row, row, row your boat, gently down the stream," I sang it over and over and over again, and as the wind grew louder, I sang louder and louder. I remembered myself as a young girl playing in the backyard with my sister, Nancy. I could see us as young girls, laughing and swinging on our swing set. Memories of who I once was started to flood into my heart, and I knew that I was going to escape. For the first time in my life, I fell to my knees and pleaded for help. It wasn't long until I received insights about how to escape --- insights that my mind had never considered. I stopped resisting him, and in time, he began bored and an opening occurred for me to escape. And, I did.

Please never forget this story. You may need it one
day to row your own boat.

When I felt it was the right time, I asked Moe how she es-
caped. She said that the escape was not the important story for
me to know. What was important was the fact that she fell to her
knees and pleaded for guidance beyond her own mind. She was
given insights and the will to carry out a plan of escape.

I still wanted to know more about the escape. She said that
the story of her escape might be helpful for others who had been
held captive, but she hoped I would learn to focus on what she
termed the life-giving story—that she had started joyfully singing, breathing, and remembering an innocent, loving time with
her sister, and she had *asked for help.* She said that when she
started to be more curious about the golden lessons rather than
the drama of life, she saw that she had been given many messages
from God that she had not even recognized.

To this day, I don't know about the escape, but I know about
her asking for help and the power of prayer. I have learned to
listen for God's voice and messages in every interaction and not
to dwell on dramatic details.

After pleading to something more than her mind in the
cabin, Moe's life went on fast-forward to learn who or what had
given her those messages. She became a student of various teachers and teachings at that time—Gay Gaer Luce, Richard Moss,
Bhagwan Shree Rajneesh (Osho), Bo Lozoff, Ram Dass, Patricia
Sun, Barbara Marx Hubbard, and eventually Joel Goldsmith and
The Infinite Way. She lived in vegetarian and vegan spiritual
communities, constantly struggling to distinguish between her
mind and the voice of God.

The teachers she was led to always encouraged her to go
within and not follow them, a teaching for which she remains

immensely grateful. She did not have a real guide until she met Barbara Thomas, whom she calls her spiritual mother. When Moe became lost in her studies of Eastern religions and the New Age, it was Barbara Thomas who took her hand and listened as Moe sifted and sorted and made sense of what she had learned to that point.

Barbara's unconditional love and deep listening helped Moe to hear her own voice and to find her own truth. Eventually, Moe became a sincere student of the teachings of Jesus and Christian mysticism.

When I met her, she was blind in one eye and had partial sight in the other. It didn't surprise me that she had received the Happy Patient award in 2008 from the University of Illinois Retina Department and eventually got more sight back. Her relentless commitment to her spiritual path is not something she needs to talk about; she lives it.

One day, Moe shared what she had written in her journal when she learned she was blind:

October, 2003 ...

Every morning when I wake up I must remember I am not blind, I am just learning to see in a new way. My practice must be to remember the part of my consciousness that lives in a place that is above, beyond, within and around this earthly dimension. This place always offers clarity and calm ... I will listen for the small voice to navigate my way through the dense fog. I will listen to the rhythms of life; I will listen to widen the inner view of what is happening around me. I will renew this practice throughout the day to make sure that

I am conscious of it. At the end of the day I will review and give thanks for another day to practice. ... and begin again. I also cannot deny that this is hard. I miss seeing the colors and textures of the world. I must learn to see another way. I will hold on to the mantra that Bo Lozoff gave me: Happy with eyesight, Happy without eye sight." I can do this, one minute, one day at a time. I can. I know I can. I have too ... I want to see while blind.

July, 2004, days before another surgery ...

Recently a friend said she was going to imagine my upcoming eye surgery as going perfectly. I thanked her. Then I asked what that would look like to her.

She immediately responded ..."your eyes are fixed and you can see clearly again." We were sitting close enough where I could sense and feel, in my own way, the tenderness of her expression. I let her love in.

While I loved the sincerity of her expression for my upcoming surgery and her tenderness, her desire for my "eyes to be fixed" is not my prayer. Although, I accept that it is hers, and I receive it. I so love all of our different ways, paths, views ...

I know my eyes are not broken. There is a divine order happening here. There is nothing to be fixed.

My retinal detachments have taken me to remember God, again and again ... deeper and deeper. Yes, I would love to access a deeper love and knowing without having to go through the doors of medicine, however, knowing that this is part of my path continues to remind me to surrender to God's will, not mine, again and again. I was told it is a straight and narrow path and the piercing of the veil is the price I must pay to see beyond the beyond.

It's not about what I want or don't want anymore. It's all about flowing in the river ... practicing my practice.

My prayer is that I can merge into whatever happens with as much grace as possible. My prayer is that I not run from what is ... that I meet it. That I meet God however God is revealed. I also want to remember a parable that I was told long ago: A woman was being chased by a group of tigers. Running, she comes to the edge of a cliff. Seeing the tigers coming after her, she knew she had to keep going, and fortunately she saw a vine going down the cliff. She clung to it and started to make her way down. She was feeling hopeful until she saw another group of tigers at the bottom of the cliff. Looking up and looking down, she saw no way out. Feeling hopeless that she would forever lose the beauty of life, she looked to the right and there was a clump of big red juicy strawberries that she could easily reach. Clinging to the vine with one hand, she took one strawberry and put it into her mouth and in those moments, she felt calm and nourished by this gift from God and was thankful for the life she had been so blessed to live.

Please God, during my hopeless moments, help me to shift my perspective. Help me to know that no matter what happens in surgery, there is always a strawberry. I just have to look and remember you are always with me, no matter what, in this surgery and always.

I know today that being led to Moe and the life coach she assigned me was and remains a blessing beyond words. I want you to know more about her because, as you will soon see, Moe along with many others helped me to meet me and to discover spiritual principles that I live by today. She also helped me see the world with new eyes and a warm heart.

My immersion into the material life had been deep. It took sitting with someone who had been through her own transformation for me to go through my own. I had no idea that the journey would turn me inside out.

Meeting Moe

DRIVING DOWN THE GRAVEL, PINE-LINED ROAD, I FELT LIKE I was entering another world. I tried to fight back tears. I wanted to appear confident, but I was scared to death. I prayed that Moe would tell me what was wrong with me and give me a very clear map to get well and fix my marriage. I wanted her place to be like my beauty shop. She would tell me what needed to be cut out and reshaped, and then she would do it. I had no idea I was entering a place where I would be required to take the long journey of discovering who I was underneath the haircut.

Moe walked out to greet me with wide-open arms. I could feel her warm welcome on this cold, dark day. My tears started to flow when she put her arm around me. As we walked through the door, I noticed a small sign that read, "We are all just walking each other home."

After she showed me my simple and modest quarters, we sat at a round oak table next to a bay window looking out on the snow-covered pines. The smell of the wood burning in the fireplace and the apple cider on the stove enveloped me in love. Moe served homemade bean and tomato soup with warm bread in dark wooden bowls. It was all so simple. I was surrounded in textures, rich earth colors, and handmade art. I was a long way away from the Emirates Palace, from the Four Seasons Hotel, and from a life of excess.

I felt like I had come home, but not to the home I was familiar with. I couldn't hide here, even if I wanted to. Every place I looked seemed to invite me to rest and stay a while. I wondered what stories the walls would tell if they could talk.

Eventually we sat by the fire. I felt safe enough in the textured, deep gold, overstuffed chair to pour my heart out. She listened. She didn't interrupt. In this space, I wanted to open the door to all my feelings and thoughts. I knew I wasn't completing my sentences as one thought ran into another, but it didn't seem to matter. I was "emptying the bowl," as she called it. Finally, I could hear my own voice and desperation. The words of John Fox express how I felt:

When Someone Deeply Listens to You
When someone deeply listens to you
it is like holding out a dented cup
you've had since childhood
and watching it fill up with
cold, fresh water.

My first visit to Moe offered me a sincere appreciation for the power of telling my story in an uninterrupted, safe space. I was invited to close my eyes, travel back in time, and paint a picture of my life up to then. I didn't need to tell my journey in chrono-logical order, there was no right or wrong way to share, and no clock was ticking. It was shocking to lean back in my chair and be told there was no time limit. Hour after hour, images and memories surfaced that I had not thought about in many years. Tears continually streamed down my cheeks. I had had no idea I had been holding on to so many emotions: hurt, anger, fear. The invitation to tell my story in this loving environment led me to new insights and awareness about my conditioned mind. Moe and the life coach simply witnessed. There were no interpretations or feedback. They were passengers on the journey with me, listening.

It got messy when we explored the concepts I was holding on to for dear life. It was frightening to hear myself speak my truth. So much of my life had been devoted to trying to please others. I wanted a Cinderella story. I wanted Prince Charming to take care of everything. I wanted a map showing me how to make sure life turned out on my terms. I wanted to control everything. Furthermore, I didn't want to go through pain or be uncomfortable.

With Moe, I shared something I haven't told you about yet. While traveling the tour, often spending hours alone in hotel rooms, I had secretly begun a search for inner peace. I realized I needed help. I knew I was stuffing my feelings and rigidly trying not to make mistakes. My mind was always critiquing every move I made. I was constantly scanning, spinning, and *trying* to be okay in everyone's eyes. I lived in constant fear of disappointing someone, especially him. I never felt I was enough. I felt tight and controlled.

I read the self-help and spiritual books that promised there was a feeling place inside ourselves that was beyond our chattering minds. In various ways, the books said that when our minds calm down, we can open an inner door to experience inner peace. It was described as a peace that is untouched by the circumstances of the outer world.

This peace eluded me, and I wanted to find it. I didn't know how. I didn't think I had ever felt inner peace. When I had gone to church as a young girl, I hadn't felt peaceful. My life was filled with people who were rushing around, always on a mission to get something accomplished. If they were pausing to watch a sunrise, I didn't see it.

Often, after he shut the door to go practice, I picked up the latest spiritual self-help book that I had purchased. I loved reading a wide array of books. I felt hopeful that a place of peace existed. When I read Christian books, I became a Christian. When I read Buddhism, I became a Buddhist. I became a Sufi. I read books about mindfulness, breathing, meditation, present-moment living, how to deal with stress, and so on. I never shared with him what I was reading, for fear that he might think I wasn't okay. Secretly, I took in concept after concept about the inner journey, but I had no idea how to apply these loving concepts in my life. Soon after I put the books down and went outside of the hotel, my thoughts became completely outer-directed.

When I finally talked about my search and asked Moe for feedback, she smiled and said she viewed my longing for inner peace as a call for a more meaningful life. I didn't believe her. I had been reading the books because I wanted out of the personal hell I was experiencing. I wanted to calm my restless mind, disentangle from the constant worry of making a mistake, and be attractive enough to him that he would never want to leave me. That's all I truly wanted. I couldn't connect a meaningful life with inner peace. I wasn't sure what a meaningful life even meant.

My life coach was assigned by Moe to reinforce what surfaced in my first intensive. The plan was that we would talk weekly on the phone about specific topics. I spent some time alone with her and felt she would be a lifeline to him and for what I was learning with Moe.

After I shared my story, Moe suggested that while my exploration of various spiritual paths showed sincerity, it was time for me to learn to walk on the earth before I gazed at the stars. Simply, she believed I had been exploring spiritual practices without a clear understanding of my core self, my true self-worth, and my unique place on the earthly plane. She suggested that I consider exploring and valuing my humanness, which included understanding what I had learned in early family dynamics and my ego, motives, and relationship patterns.

I asked her to share more about how she knew this. She leaned back and said that for most of her life, her mind had been the master. She had not had a relationship with anything bigger than her mind. At one time she also had a longing for inner peace, a calmer mind, and more meaning in her life. She too looked outside herself for this peace and met many people who offered her concepts, techniques, and theories. She learned that she did not know how to quiet her mind to hear anything more than what she had learned in the marketplace of life. She wanted to be more present in the moment but could only get little glimpses.

When she shared this, I felt safe and less inferior. She said she wanted to listen and help me sift and sort through what I was learning in the places I wanted to explore. She wanted me to hear my own voice and get to know Jocelyn. There was no other person in the world like me. Hearing these words, I softened.

I heard her say that she thought I might be trying to transcend the human plane through various spiritual practices. Perhaps I needed to enter it with a new consciousness—my own beliefs and knowing. I didn't know exactly what this meant. I did know that trying mindfully to eat one slice of an orange at a time had not helped me communicate with him. I did know that trying to meditate always ended up with me feeling bad about myself because I couldn't find the inner peace the books talked about. I did know that for most of my life, underneath all my posturing, I had rarely felt *any* inner peace.

I had been reading a little of this and a little of that, searching for refuge from my inner torment. She gently took my hand and said that she hoped I would become friends with myself. I hated that word "hoped." I wanted assurance.

I didn't know what befriending myself had to do with repairing my marriage. I became uncomfortable again. I wanted her to tell me that my marriage was going to be fixed and I was going to be okay. His coaches taught him how to hold a golf club in order to get the ball into the hole. I wanted the same instructional map. I wanted her to tell me how to fix this mess I was in.

She simply said, "Jocelyn, as you learn how to make friends with yourself, you will begin to make friends with everyone around you. In your story, I heard you describe times in your early life when you felt truly happy. Can you remember those times when you let go and let the horses carry you across the meadow with the wind on your cheeks? You weren't trying to change yourself, your horse, or the wind. You weren't trying to improve anything or prove your worth to anyone. You were at peace. You were happy with what is. Remember?"

As she said those words, I remembered. That place of peace beyond my understanding was inside me, but I had wandered far from it. I had replaced it with materialistic desires, excess, and false security. Where was God in my life?

As I told my story, I became acutely aware of my lack of self-worth and how my emotions had taken over. I was given a glimpse into the destructive power of fear and how much I had been starving for his approval and acceptance. It took a while for me to understand that my journey was one of learning to develop emotional wisdom and intelligence.

My perceptions had been clouded by my fears and insecurities.

I was beginning to understand that I had lost myself and had become an extension of him and the golf world. I needed to get to know me, Jocelyn. It took time for me to learn to observe my behavior and to understand the patterns that had kept me from knowing me.

Within a few months of my first meeting with Moe, he announced that our marriage was over. I did not know I was going to have to learn about me without him.

Divorce—Over and Out

I LOVED HIM WITH ALL MY HEART. I LOVED *HIS* HEART, HIS eyes, his smile, and his passion. He was considered one of the best in the world. I never dreamed our marriage would end in the conference room of the same hotel where we were married. I thought we were coming together for a meeting to create a plan to reignite our marriage. I did not know the flame of love for me in him was gone.

During our several months of separation, we had each intended to explore the issues that had created distance between us. I was learning about the aspects of me that I sincerely wanted to change. I was excited and felt hopeful that our marriage could be better than ever.

The meeting was in the late afternoon. I spent hours choosing a light green dress that would reflect my desire to be more feminine and engaging with him.

The small, formal, mahogany table was set with crystal water glasses, sharp pencils, and pads of paper. As we sat down across the table from each other, the hotel waitress asked if she could bring us anything. I wanted to blurt out, "Bring us back together," but I was composed. He looked so handsome, so put together. I wanted to reach across the table and squeeze his hand. But his demeanor was cold and unwelcoming, not at all what I hoped for.

I arrived hopeful and left the room utterly devastated.

I wondered how he could be so deliberate, so sure our marriage was over. No matter what I said, he did not waver in his decision. I had seen this self-assuredness on the golf course every day. I had seen him tune out sounds, crowds, wandering thoughts, and me. He knew, like all professional athletes, how to stand in the heat, and yet I knew he was a man with feelings. From the time he was learning to putt as a young boy, he was also learning not to allow his emotional life to sway him in any way. He had learned how to remain in a neutral position regarding many losses and occasional wins. He had been trained well.

But I knew his capacity to express warmth. I knew him. I thought he wanted to know me. We had experienced countless moments when love flowed between us.

I also knew on that day in the conference room, he meant what he said. This wasn't a spontaneous decision. Our marriage was completely over.

Hand in hand, we had entered into the lifestyle of the rich as we traveled around the world. We had shared loving, crazy-fun moments. We had lived together and been best friends for seven years before we married. We didn't have children, but I had dreamed of creating a family together. Divorce wasn't supposed to happen to people like us.

He leaned back from the table as he looked me in the eyes and spoke my nightmare: "I want a divorce. Our marriage is over."

His words felt calculated, practiced, and on-task. He had clearly come to the meeting to deliver my nightmare.

As you might imagine, the media immediately wanted our story, especially the drama. I would like to say we didn't have drama, but that wouldn't be true. It wasn't the type of drama that the neighbors or friends or golf coaches could see or know about. It was the drama that arrives in the night like a slithering, silent snake and hides between the sheets and in the crevices of every conversation. One day, our hidden drama slithered out of the shadows to reveal the painful truth. He didn't want to talk about it, work on it, or even tell me exactly why he wanted it all to end.

Soon after he told me, we verbally agreed not to contribute to the media's distortions and gossip. The day our divorce was official, November 11, 2011, he stated publicly in the sports section of a UK newspaper, "My career was costing Jocelyn her dreams." He didn't say that he had stopped loving me and that he felt smothered by me. He didn't say that he didn't want to work on the marriage and that I had no idea he was going to say he wanted a divorce. I know, I know—we don't often tell the whole truth.

It wasn't his career that kept me from being me. It was me who had become completely immersed in his success or failure. It was me who took care *of* him rather than caring *for* him. He never asked me to iron his shirts, lay his clothes out, pack his bags, arrange the hotels, or tend to the endless details required to ensure that he arrived at the tournament exactly on time. At that time, I thought this was what I was supposed to do. I wanted to be his wife, and these were the things I thought good wives did for their husbands. He told me he appreciated it. Later I learned he thought I was mothering him. He might have said "smothering." Are mothering and smothering one and the same? I don't know.

He was proud of my interior design talent and loved my success with my horses. As we were traveling, he assured me that we could each pursue our own careers, and our relationship could withstand some distance. I think he even said that distance makes the heart grow fonder. Somehow, I didn't believe that. Very early on, a veteran golf wife fueled my already insecure self by telling me that many gorgeous female fans were looking for any opportunity to be with a sports professional who could offer her private jets, fancy restaurants, exotic vacations, expensive clothes, and maybe, fame.

I was afraid someone else would be by his side if I wasn't with him.

I tried harder and harder to be everything for him so he wouldn't be attracted to another woman who was prettier, smarter, more accomplished, sexier, and simply better than me. I lost perspective and forgot about Jocelyn Hefner. I forgot what really matters. I eventually felt broken and disconnected from a sense of belonging anywhere.

Our meeting, marriage, and eventual parting both shattered and awakened my heart. Within days after he told me our marriage was over, I remembered my dad's voice whispering to me when I was a little girl, "No matter what, you have to get back up on the horse, Jocelyn."

But I couldn't. I went to our house and was soon curled up in a fetal position in our king-size bed. I wondered if I would ever get up. The lights went out in my life. I was done. Cooked. Hopeless.

If you have been to this place of despair, you know it's real. Despair is real. Some people might say that being curled up in an expensive bed in a multimillion dollar mansion was hardly a place of despair. I understand that viewpoint. Just hear me. Despair is despair whether you are living in luxury or are homeless on a sidewalk. Despair is deep inside and has very little to do with what things look like on the outside. There's no winning with any talks about despair. It's a dark place. It's hell. When the lights go out, it doesn't matter where you are. There is no darkness like the cave of despair.

In those moments, I learned I had nothing to hold on to. After all the expensive clothes in my closet, travels to every part of the world, meetings with famous people, and a life full of luxuries, I finally reached deep inside myself for comfort, for understanding, for hope, for refuge—and I was empty. My heart was tightly clenched, too fearful to allow the intensity of the reality of his words and actions to wash through me. I gasped for breath and became hypercritical, judging myself for not handling this the way I had handled my horse over obstacles during the most strenuous of competitions. He had known what he was doing. Standing perfectly still, with one swift stroke, he had put the ball exactly where he wanted. After all, he was one of the best.

As he packed and prepared to make his way into his new life, I was more than pathetic. Listening to him tell me that he never wanted to hurt me and he would always make sure I was okay only made me feel worse. Why couldn't he have been mean? Why couldn't he have done something to make me hate him? I wanted to be furious. Instead, I sobbed so hard I felt my eyeballs were going to fall out. I was in self-pity and deep denial.

It took me several years before I realized what denial means: you can't see what you can't see. I could not see how much I needed to be needed, whether he needed it or not.

During those days, I had no concept of what time it was, and I did not care. Popcorn and Coolwhip, our whippet pups, nuzzled me with their soft, cool noses. Of course they knew something was wrong. I didn't know how, in those days, to be with *our* precious dogs. I had been the one to bring the whippets into our lives, but the memory of him being close to each of them remained so clear.

In fact, memories were everywhere. When I made my way to the bathroom, there was the tile we had picked out together because it had the right shade of gray. In the kitchen was the coveted coffee machine that was his Holy Grail. Was he going to take it? Why was it still there? I didn't want to see it. It hurt too much. All I could remember was how much he loved his espresso in a small, white, Italian cup and how he smiled when I brought it to him along with his favorite biscotti.

How could he have forgotten all that I had done for him? How could he throw all those moments away? But he did. He really, really did. He was gone. I felt like ending it all by simply getting in my fancy car and driving off a cliff. I couldn't imagine not being with him. My time with Moe seemed like a distant dream.

My life coach was hired to live with me and be on twenty-four-hour watch. I finally admitted that I needed someone who knew me well enough to help me through my despair. My life coach knew of my insecurities. She knew of my private self. She didn't buy into the confident image I had pulled off in the media. She knew his leaving had the power to dismantle all of my illusions, shatter my heart, and reveal that I had nothing to hold on to except, maybe, her. I knew my family would hold my hand, but I couldn't burden them by asking them to hold my broken heart.

I know it's only the rich who can hire a residential life coach. While I am grateful, I wish I hadn't needed that level of help. They could have put me in a psych ward and medicated me into zombie land. Then I could have written a victim story talking about him abandoning me. It didn't happen that way. I had to feel my despair, face my shadows, and wake up.

My coach was my lifeline who helped me get through those dark, lonely nights. Gradually, she helped me to help myself get back on the horse. She helped me to stay with my fear and pain and open up to the weight of my loss.

Never in my life had I stayed with painful feelings surging like a tsunami through my body. It wasn't that I was strong; it was that no one was rescuing me. By being forced to stay with my despair, for the first time I started to connect with my inner life. I learned how empty I was, how lost. I had never allowed myself to touch the hot flames of true feelings. I had created a life in which I didn't have to feel my feelings. I had always moved forward, away from anything or anyone who might shine a light on my true self. The woman he had met and loved had become small, had given up all her dreams to be with him, and was carrying a hole in her soul for betraying her own heart.

Why had I bypassed his encouragement to follow my interests and passions? Why for so many years had I said yes when I wanted to say no and no when I wanted to say yes? Why had the fear of not being enough taken control my life?

The journey to answer these questions took me to places and people that previously only existed for me in movies and books. I met people from all walks of life who had also found themselves in utterly despairing places and had burned through the fire to find the joy of our common humanity.

I met people who were willing to talk about their human flaws and how they returned to their true selves. I met a woman who dropped out of a highly acclaimed graduate school because she heard a deeper call to her heart. She couldn't help but join a volunteer program helping abused women. I met others who dropped out of the corporate world to live their dreams. One man, who made a lot of money but hated his job, sold everything for a happier life in which he could take photographs of nature.

I listened to their stories. I cried with them and laughed with them. Slowly, their sharing transformed my previous conceptions about how life and love are supposed to work.

I began to see life as earth school. My hunger to know more

created a shift in perception that changed everything. The PGA and European tours became one of my classrooms for learning about the complexities of fame, friendships, ambition, money, hunger to succeed, triumphs, failure, integrity, balance, infidelity, exhaustion, anger, loyalty, and how the hunt for fame and love was always in season, and yet somehow always eluded me.

When I began to view relationships as teachers, he became my master teacher. Our differing definitions of love took me to my knees and eventually allowed me to open the door to living the life I was meant to live.

My journey has made me want to live a life that offers me pauses—sunrises in the morning and the moon's light at night. I want a life that reflects caring about what feels right and just and good, a life that includes loving everyone, no matter what.

He and all the pro golfers and their partners have taught me more about love than I could ever have imagined. This is my way of giving back and showing that we are not our pasts. Our purposes lie in the present.

The Inward Journey

So it was. I was living in a gorgeous, immaculate house. He was gone. The life we had created together was over. My fear of not being enough and losing him had come true. He promised there wasn't another woman; I was not a "bad wife"; it wasn't my fault. I didn't believe him. It didn't matter.

It wasn't until I was confronted with losing him that I confronted reality and awakened to the emptiness of my inner life. Our divorce was made real by him moving out. Curled up in the fetal position, I scrutinized all my flaws. I couldn't see one thing right about me. The idea of befriending myself and finding any peace seemed very far away.

I didn't tell my friends what had happened. I believed it wasn't important to them anyway. All I wanted was for him to come back and try to work it out. I replayed over and over and over again our meeting, our years together, how much fun we had traveling around the world, and how much I loved him. In the night, I found myself reaching for him. Why hadn't I reached for him before? Why hadn't I realized that marriage can end? What was wrong with me?

It was Moe who took my hand and assigned me to the life coach who lived with me for many months and helped me return to aliveness again. When the coach moved in with me, as an alternative to sending me out to a psych ward, I could barely lift my head. My heart was broken. My skin was turned inside out. I didn't know what to do, where to go, or how to live without him. I felt disconnected from everything I thought was vital and meaningful.

I didn't want the divorce, yet I hadn't put up a good fight or tried to convince him otherwise. As usual, I was doing whatever he wanted. If he wanted his freedom and didn't want to be with me, I wasn't going to do anything to prevent him from fulfilling his life dreams. I didn't tell him how I really felt. I didn't ask many questions. I completely folded.

I hate that I didn't fight. While I don't think it would have done any good, at least I could have gotten some anger out. I know depression is anger turned inward. I think depression is worse than anger.

What I have to share now happened over a period of a couple of years. It was a process and a journey. I can't give you the whole picture, but I hope the glimpses that I can give you will be of help with your own journeys.

The Long Nights and Long Days

IT TOOK A LONG TIME FOR ME TO UNDERSTAND OUR PARTING had nothing to do with me not being a loving partner or person. I gradually recognized the tremendous tension that had accumulated as a result of living in fear of losing him. In my healing journey after the divorce, I began to untie the knots that blocked my receptivity to my heart.

Lying in bed, it felt like a thousand voices were in my head, all of them screaming that I failed. I hadn't done it right. I hadn't done enough. I had done too much. I was pathetic. I remember wanting Moe and my coach to tell me I had not failed. "Please tell me he was a jerk." While anger did not surface at this time, I gave myself permission to be angry.

Over time, I talked about how I felt. No advice was offered except to stay with the pain. Moe listened and whispered, "Tell me more." I talked and sobbed at the same time. I pleaded to have my life back.

It was during the hours and days of pleading that something shifted within me. I can't explain it. I started to surrender. My coach compassionately took my hand and said, "We will make our way. I can't do this for you, but Moe and I can be *with* you."

Accepting What Is

I FINALLY LOOKED IN THE BATHROOM MIRROR. THE FACE I saw was not the face I knew. It was of a woman who had been blindsided. As I continued to look, I remembered all the quotations I had read in self-help books that said that for love to be real, it must hurt. For the first time, I got a glimpse of what this meant. I had to go through the pain of getting to know and love myself.

Standing in front of the mirror was a moment that inspired me to align myself to the truth of what is. I had to blaze a new trail. In my reading, I had encountered others' stories of going through the dark night of the soul. Now it was my turn.

When he finally closed the door, I fired the cleaning crew. I put the vacuum cleaner in the garage and drove myself to the barn. It felt like everything was in slow motion as I made my way to the stalls. It was late afternoon and no one else was around; it was me and my horses. The smells and fresh air reminded me that I had a life to live—a new life. When I went back home, I hugged Coolwhip and Popcorn for the first time in weeks. I had missed them and they had missed me.

Finally, I was ready to do the best I could to accept what had happened and what was happening. I didn't want to die as "one who almost lived."

I had been working with my coach for some time by then. She knew me. She knew the people-pleasing, materialistic, jealous, rigid part of me. She also knew that, underneath the "I will do anything for you to love me" behavior, I was smart, sincere, organized, loving, compassionate, passionate, funny, competent, strong, and most of all, willing to look at myself and not see myself as a victim. Had I not felt my feelings during this time and emptied out so much suffering, I am not sure I could have gotten back up. I was a mess.

I had never, ever experienced this level of suffering, let alone felt the feelings. My suffering penetrated because there were no buffers. No one offered me false hope or told me I was going to be okay. No one tried to tame my wild mind, my tears, my sadness, or my despair. I was not rescued from the heat of pain. Knowing my precious dogs were near helped me realize I wasn't alone.

At one point, my coach reminded me I was with all the people in the world who were suffering and with all the people who were opening a door to a new way of living. She read an excerpt from the book *The Heart of the Buddha's Teaching: Transforming Suffering into Peace, Joy and Liberation* by Thích Nhất Hạnh, a Vietnamese monk: "The seed of suffering in you may be strong, but don't wait until you have no more suffering before allowing yourself to be happy."

I didn't understand why anyone would ever embrace suffering. It took time for me to understand it was in this suffering that I would eventually start to connect with my inner life, my feelings, and the real Jocelyn. There were many steps on the journey for me to understand the value of embracing suffering.

I was reluctant to go back to Moe because by now I was convinced that she wasn't going to try to teach me anything. She only shared, offered, and suggested that I explore and consider possibilities. She definitely would not try to "fix" me nor offer false refuge for relief. There was no way she was going to disempower me by creating any dependence on her.

Moe's commitment to everyone finding a direct relationship with the higher power of their understanding never shifted. Initially, this was intimidating. I gradually learned that she believed that any person, place, or thing that gets between ourselves and the God of our understanding eventually will block us from knowing our truth. Blockage creates dependencies. She asked a lot of exploratory questions, and sometimes I didn't feel like exploring my feelings. It would have been much easier to turn on the television or go to a beauty spa.

One of the most significant questions Moe suggested was to ask myself if the pain I was feeling was in part created by a conflict between what was and what I wanted life to be. My first reaction was to tell her the question was irrelevant. Of course I wanted things to be different. I didn't want a divorce.

However, after I expressed my frustration, I entered a long pause. In the pause, I saw the value of her question and admitted it was true. I did not want to accept his leaving. I didn't want what was. Until I did, I would suffer. He was gone. That was the truth. I had to accept it.

However, I couldn't seem to stop the constant internal question of why he didn't want to work on our marriage. Why couldn't he give me time to work on the ugly parts of myself? Why weren't we talking about his role in all of this? Was it *all* me? I wasn't all wrong, all bad—was I?

When I asked these questions out loud, all I heard was my own voice. It was very powerful. There was no advice or storyline speculating on the answers. No interruptions. Simply, no one was getting on the anxiety merry-go-round of unanswerable questions with me. All I heard was, "What is the next single thing you need to do in order to find you own answers and inner wisdom?"

I knew that answer: Get up. Brush my teeth. Take care of the dogs. Hire a lawyer. Start to face the inevitable realities that come with ending one way of life and creating another.

Moe asked if I was ready to end the relationship and follow through with the divorce. Tears flowed down my face. When I could catch my breath, I shared that it was not in my heart to let him go so easily, so effortlessly. I wrote down everything I was feeling. Then I wrote him a letter, asking if he was really done with our marriage. I thought I would give it one last chance, even though I knew he meant what he had said.

Waiting for a response was like waiting for a life-or-death lab result. It was so unsettling that I decided to create some distraction by changing my outer appearance. I imagined a fantasy that if I looked better, everything would be okay.

Altering my looks was not new to me. Through the years I had made physical parts smaller, bigger, slimmer, and smoother. Some of these alterations had been for me, but most were made to make me more attractive to others. I did not know if the alterations would help, but other women told me they would.

I had absolutely no awareness of how much I relied on the words and suggestions of others until I got hair extensions.

I will always remember getting the extensions glued to my head while sitting in my room in the Chicago Four Seasons Hotel. My dogs were on the bed and music was playing in the background. When I looked in the mirror after three hours, I hated them.

However, I didn't want to hurt the beautician's feelings. So I faked it and acted as if I liked them. When she left, I immediately put my long hair in a ponytail. I was amazed in that moment at how far I would go not to hurt others' feelings or to keep them from knowing my truth.

The next day I went to a hair salon to get the extensions cut and shaped into a style. Unfortunately, that didn't work either. I felt like I looked like an exercise instructor from the 1980s. I felt ugly. I was mad at myself for ever starting all of this in the first place.

Next on the agenda was a pedicure, which in the past had always made me feel better. This time was different.

While in the pedicure chair, I received a text reply from him to my letter. His response was direct. He said he was not interested in understanding the demise of our marriage or learning from it.

I gasped. The nail technician did not know what to say when I burst into tears. I felt like throwing up.

Instead, I went home, ripped out my hair extensions, and booked another intensive with Moe.

Taking One Step at a Time

AGAIN I WENT TO SEE MOE AND WAS GREETED WITH A warm hug and a bowl of soup at the round table. After I settled in, it was clear that this time my intensive would be different. We needed to move into the source of the psychological turbulence in which I had been living. I was reminded that my staying with my suffering had opened the door to the inner chambers of my heart, where healing lies.

We began with a thorough inventory of how I had built a protective wall around my heart for fear of not being enough. Hour after hour I revisited significant times in my childhood when I tried to control the uncontrollable in order to shield myself from pain and discomfort. With this inventory, I clearly saw how I had learned to avoid pain in intimate relationships by staying on the periphery of conversations so I wouldn't say anything "wrong." I learned at an early age to react quickly rather than be willing to rest in a pause and respond with my truth. I saw how I had not learned to be compassionate and loving toward myself. The written and spoken inventory offered me a new understanding about how, without this love for me, it was difficult for me to genuinely feel love for others.

While Moe doesn't offer labels, she said it might be helpful for me to explore "codependency." I had heard this term before. She explained that it was not a pathological diagnosis, Simply, learning about the characteristics of codependency might help me in my return to my real self.

It was challenging for me to look at this. I had honestly thought I was being a helpful and good person. I hated learning that I had been taking care *of* him rather than genuinely caring *for* him. I also began to understand my hypervigilance and inability to relax around people. Because so much of my happiness was dependent on people liking me, I was always watching what I said and how I said it, terrified of offending anyone.

I felt lost. For so long I had seen myself as an extension of him, the golf world, and our material assets. It was true. I had lost myself. At the time I didn't know that most people have to become lost in order to find and return to their true selves.

It was at this time that I asked Moe if she would share more of her story. She handed me a story that she had written about a time in her life when she was lost too.

Tell Me More

I couldn't find that place within me that everyone said was a quiet place where inner wisdom resides. They said that after all their seeking they finally turned within and found what they were looking for. I loved the "idea" of this. It felt right that the answers are within me, but I couldn't find me. Not only was I unsure how to make the turn within, I didn't have the energy; I was exhausted.

In desperation I went to see a counselor. His name was Rudy, and he specialized in depression. A couple of people said he might be able to be helpful and yet, as I made my way to his office, I didn't feel hopeful or discouraged. I just climbed the stairs and sat in the dimly lit empty waiting room. I was glad there were no papers to fill out because I might have written that I have no name, no home (I was sleeping on my friend's couches) and no life.

Rudy greeted me with a warm handshake and guided me to the blue speckled living room-like chair next to the window in his office. I didn't care where I sat. I glanced out the window and immediately noticed a small gray bird sitting on the limb of the Juniper tree. Rudy noticed that I saw it and sat quietly with me. It was as if somehow we both knew the importance of pausing for beauty.

As we sat there, together, tears started to stream down my cheeks and gradually touch my lips. As the little bird jumped to another branch, I whispered, "I'm so lost. I don't know who I am anymore. I can't find any meaning, and I don't know where to go or what to do." The bird moved slightly and Rudy continued to remain silent. I could feel him listening. Others had tried to listen, but in a different way. Rudy just sat watching the bird and listening. He didn't offer any knowing or philosophies. He didn't say he could help m or that he had ideas or possible solutions.

I began to tell him the story --- how I had once been an administrator at a major university. I had made lots of money, walked with authority, and had great form to my life in my Evan Picone tailored suits worn with suntan nylons and perfect pumps. I had a name, a reputation, high academic credentials, a beautiful home, husband, child, friends and a big, worldly life. Now, I was sitting in his office with nothing except the story of my past. I couldn't find a reason to live.

His silence continued as I shared how it all had happened --- how I had resigned from my tenured university position and hit the road to find out if there really was a God. On and on I shared how I felt I had lost my life. Rudy remained silent until he finally whispered, "Just tell me more; tell me all of it." There didn't seem to be a clock ticking, he wasn't looking at his watch, he hadn't asked how I was going to pay for the session and he hadn't told me his credentials. He simply said, "Tell me more. I want to hear all of it." Hearing these words, the floodgate of my heart was invited to open, and I could finally tell it all, and at the same time, hear myself. The bird kept pausing, jumping to another branch, and staying right with us. "Tell me more."

It was only much later that I learned I had been in his office for over three hours. Finally, I said, "I am too tired to tell you anymore." He responded by asking if I wanted to come back soon. For the first time in months I felt the "Yes" inside me.

The little gray bird flew away as I made my way out of his office. I walked down the hill a bit more hopeful. He didn't tell me I had post-traumatic stress syndrome.

He didn't give me a label or suggest I go on medication. He honored my own knowing by listening and not interrupting. Finally, I could hear my own story without having to hear his. Although I didn't know if there are fully enlightened people on the earthly plane, I do believe I was the recipient of enlightened action.

This went on for several weeks: Tell me more Moe, and I did. And I began to see how the path had led me to this point. His caring silence helped me to empty out my story, my pain, my longing, so I could begin to make that turn to my own wisdom voice again.

Rudy never charged me for our sessions. Perhaps he remembered a time in his own life when

someone gave the holy silence to him. I promised
to pay forward deep listening in my life ...

It was pure, simple, uninterrupted space to empty
out the stories that no longer served my life.

Moe also shared that at one time she had attended codependency twelve-step meetings, and had learned more in the meetings than in any book anyone could have offered her.

Feelings

I DIDN'T KNOW IF I FELT LIKE ATTENDING CODEPENDENCY meetings. I was beginning to see that for most of my life, I hadn't known how I felt. I often knew what I thought, but I did not know how I felt. As we explored the patterns that had kept me from knowing how I felt, I learned to respond rather than to react quickly. I practiced pausing and moving into my heart to connect with a feeling. It was jolting to learn my true feelings were layered underneath the voices of "you *should* feel this way about that." How did I, Jocelyn, feel without the voices telling me I *should* feel a certain way?

One morning I looked at my coach and told her it felt like I was beginning a journey of a thousand miles, and I felt hopeless. I was grateful when she shared it was not uncommon, especially in America, to escape painful feelings. We laughed that at least I wasn't an alcoholic, drug addict, or food binger. I was a people-pleaser, and I needed to attend codependency meetings. I was amazed at how much I learned in those twelve-step meetings.

Codependents Anonymous

IN THE MEETINGS, I LEARNED TO IDENTIFY WHAT WERE termed "shadow behaviors." I began to understand that I had lived most of my life in fear. While I had said this before, in the meetings I *felt* my fear—of people thinking I wasn't perfect, smart enough, pretty enough, or good enough. I *felt* how afraid I had been that he would leave me for another woman. I had been afraid I wouldn't be the best in a horse competition. I had been afraid I wouldn't belong if I didn't have the right clothes, shoes, purses, and accessories.

A clear example was the way I would lay out his clothes on the bed every morning of a tournament, while he took a shower. He never asked me to do this. I revisited my doing this and other things, like ironing his blue shirts. I saw I hadn't wanted to do either of those things. Nor had he ever asked me to. I did them so he would think I was an awesome girlfriend, give me praise, and never leave me. Besides, I didn't have anything else to do when he was in the shower. His life became my life.

Standing on its own, these behaviors of mine didn't have to become serious issues. They could have been resolved with honest communication. But as we reviewed my life, I could see how they reflected the larger issue of my love-starved behavior.

Identifying where I had been codependent in my life brought up many feelings of shame and guilt. However, I was learning the feelings wouldn't kill me. I could finally name the feeling, own my behavior, and see how I needed to let go of the excruciating judgment of myself. It took a while before "letting go" meant giving it to God.

It was enlightening to learn that twelve-step programs are spiritual. The twelve-steps emphasize the God of your understanding. They say that we are powerless over addictions and must ask God for help.

First, I had never thought of myself as codependent. Second, I didn't know there were support groups for this issue. Was codependency an addiction? A woman shared with me that it was a "process addiction," which I think meant it was about my thinking and people-pleasing behavior rather than about a substance. The definition she gave of addiction was very clear: "If you do something, and it creates problems in your life, and you continue to do it—it might be an addiction."

At this stage of my understanding, it all felt confusing. I was advised not to try to understand, just to go to my first meeting.

When I made my way to my first CODA meeting, I didn't know what to expect. First of all, I could not have cared less how I looked, and that was very different for me. Prior to this, I had always made sure that I looked as good as I could. I cared a lot about how people saw me, as you well know by now. I prayed I wouldn't meet anyone I knew in there, or someone who knew I was his wife. These thoughts were making me very uncomfortable, but I was in pain.

When I walked into the room, I was asked if this was my first meeting. I nodded. I didn't look anyone in the eye. I was offered information on the characteristics of codependency. I read, "If you are nice rather than honest, this support group may be for you." I knew I had always tried to be nice, but I had never thought about being nice in relationship to honesty. The definition of codependency had my name written all over it.

We sat in a circle. Each person shared his or her experience of how being codependent had affected their lives and relationships. But speaking wasn't required. I was grateful I didn't have to say anything. When it was my turn, I simply said, "Pass." Tears streamed down my cheeks almost the entire time.

Every single person said something I could relate to. The love in the room was palpable. I noticed a sign that I have never forgotten: "Don't Think." It was true. As soon as I started to think about him, I could easily drown in a pool of despair.

When I left the meeting, I knew I would be back. I knew I was with a group of people who, just like me, wanted to learn how to be kind without being codependent. I was with people who wanted to become whole. By sharing stories in these confidential meetings, I deepened in the understanding of my own story. I admitted that I had been naive, ignorant, and foolish. It was liberating to feel such an intimate connection with other people—and with myself—in such a short period of time. Gradually, my co-dependent behavior was unveiled for others to see, and everyone in the room understood.

One woman told a joke that I will never forget. She said, "If a codependent is drowning, someone else's life will flash in front of them rather than their own." I loved the humor about it all, as well as the sincerity of the desire for illusions to break open so we could be real with ourselves and the people around us. I was and remain so grateful for these meetings and to all the people who opened their hearts, told their stories of recovery, and worked the twelve-steps. I suspect everyone would benefit by experiencing what it's like to talk about their humanness without shame.

Somewhere in school I learned that Michelangelo said he saw something of beauty in a block of stone and began to chip away at everything in front of the beauty. I think that's what I was beginning to do.

Impulse Training—
Activating the Senses

ANOTHER PRACTICE I WAS WORKING ON AT THIS TIME WAS
expressing my true feelings in a direct and honest way. I asked
my coach for what we called an "intentional meeting" to discuss
one topic. I planned out what I wanted to say, but by the time we
had the meeting, I blurted out, "I am sick to death of constantly
being corrected!" She smiled, paused, and said she was tired too.
Then we burst out laughing and hugged each other.

My body braced when she took my hands, looked me tenderly
in the eyes, and told me that I needed to increase my commitment to focusing on what I was learning and practicing in order
to get where I wanted to be in my life. When I heard those words,
I immediately thought of golf coaches and how they repeatedly
said to keep one's eye on the goal.

It was true. My mind still wandered all over. I realized it
in the CODA meetings. Someone would share a tear-jerking

story from her life, and while I looked present, sometimes my mind wandered to what we were going to make for dinner that night. Once I even went so far as to make a mental grocery list while someone was talking. I hated it when I did that. I didn't do it all the time, but I did it a lot. I had no clue how to lasso my wild mind and truly be present. I didn't know how to focus on what was happening in the moment, to implement all that I was learning. Could people stay completely present if they were living in the world? I could see how they might do it if they were sitting in a cave, but I didn't see how it was possible otherwise.

Thinking these thoughts led me to the image of how present golfers were on the course. I remembered talking to a pro golfer who told me his quiet time, every day, was critical to his success. Looking back, I regret not asking him more about his quiet time practice.

Moe and my coach suggested that, in addition to reading codependency books, attending meetings, identifying and giving voice to my feelings, accepting, and detaching, it was time to discuss body and calm-mind training.

The body part was fairly easy for me since I loved to work out and eat well. Being on the tour, I had learned a lot about the importance of paying attention to what the body needed for endurance and strength. However, I had never paid attention to the five senses: smell, sight, hearing, taste, and touch. I saw how I bypassed my senses and went on automatic.

I loved noticing the quality of light in the various rooms of the house. I loved hearing the hum of the refrigerator. I loved learning to scan my body mentally from the top of my head all the way to my toes. The purpose was to practice being aware of the different sensations in different parts of my body. This seemed like common sense, but I had never taken the time to do it in a focused way. I was learning how to be present for the first time in my life.

During breakfast, we practiced staying very present to the color, texture, smell, and taste of our food. Doing this, I realized how often I had eaten my food without even tasting or appreciating it. As I dipped my silver spoon into oatmeal and raspberries, I saw the swirling red juice making love with the cinnamon and the warm almond milk. I don't think I had ever swished food around in my mouth this way to taste all the flavors. Oatmeal never tasted so good.

After breakfast we took a walk with the pups. I learned to observe what was around us more closely. At one point I stopped and watched a cloud move across the sky. I caught the fragrance of the rose garden and realized how long it had been since I had simply taken a walk without worrying about whether people were watching me.

Throughout the day, I tried to incorporate staying present in daily activities like brushing my teeth, washing the dishes, and driving the car. I can't tell you how many times I have driven somewhere and not even remembered the journey. I saw how so much of my life had been on automatic pilot, also known as "mindless." I think it was because my mind was full of thoughts about the past and worries about the future.

I also learned how often my mind wanted to race away from the present moment. I would start eating faster, stuffing my food into my mouth. My racing mind was only going to settle down if I made a deep commitment to the practice of being present.

Emptying the Bowl

MOE ENCOURAGED ME TO DO A DAILY MENTAL DETOXIFICA-tion that she called "emptying the bowl." For five minutes every morning, noon, and early evening I spoke out loud all the thoughts streaming through my mind. I did this alone, in what I called my detox chair. "Elephant. I miss him. I am uncomfortable. My arm itches. Spinach. I wish I was married. Arm still itching. I don't like doing this ..." Silence. "I want some peanut butter." On and on for five minutes. It was difficult. I felt vulnerable, exposed, and silly. However, it wasn't long until I began to see the value of it. By releasing all my random thoughts, I was making room for the inner journey to my heart, where the mind is not the master.

I learned this was a stepping-stone for learning to witness and detach from my wandering thoughts. I wanted to learn meditation right away because so many people said it was the door to inner peace. Moe suggested that we start with moving meditations because my mind was still wrestling with all that had happened and was happening. She said that "emptying the bowl" was a form of active meditation because of the focused attention on emptying out accumulated thoughts.

I was in awe of all the thoughts floating through my mind in a matter of seconds. Emptying the bowl was beginning to feel like an important part of my day. "I hate the lawyer. I want ice cream. The dogs need to go to the vet. Why did he leave? My body aches. I miss music. Hate my hair. What is he doing right now?"

In addition to the verbal throwing up (as I called it), I started doing stream-of-consciousness writing. I would sit in a quiet place with my journal and simply empty all my thoughts out on paper. I didn't pay attention to punctuation or my handwriting. It didn't need to make sense. I would simply empty every thought on paper. If I wanted to, I could tear up the paper. I usually did, with vengeance. Finally, my anger was beginning to surface.

The next emptying-out moving meditation was the most fun: dynamic meditation. I was instructed to dance to wild drumming music. In an unencumbered space, we blasted music so loud I couldn't help but want to move every inch of my body. It took a while for me to let go. Twirling. Jumping. Shaking. Laughing. I was out of my mind and into my body at last.

When the drumbeats suddenly stopped, I closed my eyes. I sat down on the floor in the middle of what felt like a tornado of twirling energy. Soothing music softly played as I inhaled and exhaled. I melted into a place where there were very few thoughts. I sensed the sound of a long, deep breath in and a long, deep breath out, the continuous life-force rhythm. Tears often rolled down my cheeks. I was changing. I was healing. Every once in a while a little smile crossed my face.

I was beginning to understand the many different forms of focused attention. There was so much for me to empty out during the day. I danced; I wrote; I emptied the bowl. The more

I emptied out, the more present I became. I was less in the past or the future.

We took walks. Slowly, I started to eat healthy food again. When I spoke with Moe about this, she shared that John Robbins, author of the book *Diet for a New America,* had told her that conscious, healthy eating included being aware of the love put into the food. I thought about all the times I had prepared and eaten food without giving any thought to how my emotions affected my food or food intake.

My coach helped me to notice when my body and thoughts were constricting and when I was expanding. I was starting to do more than understand; I was actually experiencing the journey to a quiet place of inner calm.

We began going out in Scottsdale, other than to meetings. On our first stop, the owner of my favorite restaurant asked me where my husband was playing next. At the grocery store, a mutual friend asked about him. At the horse barn, the car dealership, the gas station, the dry cleaners, the dog groomers, they asked about him. His heartbeat and footprint were everywhere.

One time while I was eating lunch in a sports bar, there he was, bigger than life, playing golf on the television screen behind the bar. Memories were everywhere in Scottsdale. Would I ever not care? I had to learn to care about other things and continue to tame my wild, wandering, chattering mind. It was time to learn about the importance of my breath and how it helped calm my entire being.

Deep Breathing

WHEN WE BEGAN TO TALK ABOUT THE IMPORTANCE OF THE breath, I knew we were entering a very important topic. Many times I have read about how deep breathing can quiet wandering minds, open hearts, and lead to mental discipline. I knew this was core work that I had been resisting. It was increasingly important to me to truly get a handle on how much my mind was ruling my life.

When I spoke with Moe about this, she shared some of her own experiences with deep breathing. She reminded me that because the breath is fresh every second, it helps the mind return to the present moment.

As usual, I learned there is no one right way to breathe. I chose to learn the deep belly breath. As I inhaled, my belly extended, and as I exhaled, my belly moved toward my spine as far as it could go. I was encouraged to take the longest breaths I could in this manner, but not to allow myself to get light-headed. It was important to feel my breath each time. It was helpful to lasso my mind by thinking, "Breathing in and breathing out."

I was amazed at how quickly my mind settled down with this one simple exercise. For most of my life, I had been advised to hold my stomach in, so this was a major departure from my tight, shallow breathing. Moe showed me a simple visual of the inward and outward flow. I saw how this continuous life-force rhythm was in many ways rocking me, in and out, creating a secure feeling.

Blood on the Highway

I HAVE NEVER FORGOTTEN THIS STORY MOE SHARED WITH me from her writings:

> I met her on the edge of the narrow gravel road. She was lying just to the left of where the semi had missed the curve and smashed into her medium-sized canary yellow sports car. Despite my friends warning that I might be involved in a lawsuit if I touched her, it wasn't the first time a quiet moaning had claimed my heart and mind. I wasn't a tourist. A lawsuit would not stop me. As her cries increased, I entered a place beyond thoughts --- miles from the harshness of daily affairs. Blood on a highway requires going beyond the mind. It is an attribute of the heart. Long before this accident I had discovered how to follow the path with

heart and allow life to grant me wisdom in ways I sometimes did not understand or choose.

Underneath the already crusting, brownish-red blood, I could see her eyelashes slowly trying to blink. Her thin lips were quivering. Instinctively, I slowly knelt down next to her and whispered that an ambulance would be arriving soon. I knew that wasn't enough; it couldn't be. I had to hold her. When I laid down and gently wrapped her bloody body in my arms, I was with her. It wasn't until later that I saw how her gushing blood had penetrated through my once green tee shirt.

I knew to be gentle in this fragile in-between place; however, she wasn't so gentle. Her fingers slowly started to dig into my upper arm as she pulled her body closer and closer to mine. It felt like she wanted to enter my body and grab my life force that was quickly fading from her once vital being. Or was she vital before the accident? I knew nothing about her.

I didn't know her name, her age, whether she was a mother or a grandmother. I didn't know if she had a college degree, where she lived, or if she was tall or short. I only knew her heart was beating like mine, and she was breathing. Her bloody hand was gripping my hand. Nothing mattered except our connection. Time was suspended, everyday life struggles, gone. There we were, on the edge of the highway, lying in a pool of blood on the edge between life and death. We were in sacred space.

"Keep breathing with me, the ambulance is coming ... your life is not over ... you have a life to live ... breathe." As I whispered these words, I knew they would fall empty if I had not been such a sincere student learning to consciously breathe from a deep place in my belly.

I could hear the sirens coming --- police cars, the ambulance, and a fire truck. I reminded her once again that they were close, and she just needed to focus on the in and out of her breathing. The breath --- the continuous life force. The sirens were comforting, yet alarming. Holding her, consciously breathing in and breathing out, she murmured, Thank you. I could feel her reaching for her breath as she felt the waves of breath in my body.

They needed to arrive, but my heart wasn't ready to let go of her. I wasn't ready to see her bloody body strapped to a gurney and rolled into the back of an ambulance with blaring sirens. I wanted her to live.

As they pealed her from my arms, I felt as if part of my breath was going with her. I asked if I could get into the ambulance, but instead was required to give a detailed report to the policeman who was standing nearby with his clipboard full of questions.

Watching the ambulance make its way down the highway with the siren blaring is a memory etched in my heart. I wanted someone to hold her, breathe with her and keep whispering that she mattered, her breath mattered.

When I learned she died in the ambulance before she reached the hospital, I vowed to remember the sacred place we held together, that place that was revealed with each conscious breath.

After I read this story, I wondered if I could do what Moe had done. My first barrier would be the fear of holding the woman and being called into a lawsuit. My second barrier was even greater—could I breathe deeply and stay calm? I wanted to be able to. I wanted to learn about breathing into the deep place within me.

I started out doing this for a few minutes throughout the day. Sometimes my mind would wander after thirty seconds, and I would forget what I was doing. The instant I remembered, I dropped the thoughts and went back to my belly-breathing practice.

On my journey, I met a woman who said that when she did this kind of breathing, she silently expressed a prayer: "May all beings find their way." I love that.

It was heartwarming to learn that though my mind quieted down, most people agreed that it was impossible for the mind to be completely quiet. I was reassured that if I stayed with this practice, my mind would stop wandering around so much and my awareness in life would be increased. I can tell you now, this is absolutely true. I have diligently practiced this breathing, and it has helped calm my mind. I can see life from a new perspective—a perspective of learning through pain rather than resisting it.

It took a long time for me to understand that I was doing these practices to tame my mind. I was starting to feel more alive than ever. Staying present with what I was doing and what was in front of me was hard, but I experienced immediate relief from thinking so much. My wandering, chattering mind had needed these practices for many years. Being present in the moment felt like a miracle, even if for a few seconds.

I couldn't imagine not thinking very much while listening to someone, but I wanted to.

There were many opportunities to stay with the in-and-out breath when someone was speaking. With very sincere and deliberate practice, gradually I found I was deeply listening to what people said, without my mind wandering. I truly focused. I saw how "multitasking" had kept me from a calmer life.

I also deepened my understanding that the purpose of my spiritual practices was to expand my heart and view of the world. My earthly struggles were not purposeless. I could learn something from every interaction in life. This is earth school, and the curriculum isn't always easy or immediately joyful. "May all beings find their way."

Emotional Debris

ALTHOUGH I PRACTICED ALL THESE TEACHINGS EACH DAY, thoughts of him were still lurking, especially at night. I cried. I missed him. I missed us. Releasing the tears alone in the dark of night was strangely comforting. I still cared.

I couldn't believe he was gone. Our life was gone. Almost every day for the last ten years, I had woken up with a purpose: packing for a tournament, being at a tournament, processing the tournament, playing with the dogs, making travel arrangements. I might have been unhappy, but my days had meaning. I had goals, places to go, and a reason to live.

One time I noticed I was feeling impatient and agitated while standing in line at Whole Foods. I wanted to scream for no particular reason. I swallowed this sudden impulse, paid for my groceries, and forgot all about it. That is, until I noticed how judgmental I was becoming. Often I wanted to snap at everyone. At first I thought it was connected to my hormones, but I soon learned that I had opened the door to all the anger I had swallowed and repressed.

It was suggested that the emotional debris I had tried to control since I was a little girl might be surfacing. There was a divine timing in life, and clearing the emotional debris was organic. We couldn't make it happen. I realized I needed to consider the clearing as another sacred passage on my journey.

I was curious about all of this, so I researched the different ways such clearing was done. Once again I was introduced to many different avenues. On the Internet, there were so many programs, techniques, books, and classes for emotional release that my head spun.

I was eager to get healthier, so I made my way back to Moe. She invited me to remember that my heart would reveal what steps were right for me. I stopped trying to figure out how the emotional debris was going to be removed. I trusted it would dissolve in proportion to my commitment to returning to my soft place of refuge within, where my inner wisdom lay. My breath would lead me. Being aware of my breathing led me to the peaceful place where I could begin again.

As we sat at the round table, Moe suggested that it was time for me to stop seeking what I already knew. It was time for me to live what I knew. When she said those words, I felt the breakthrough to the next level of loving myself. The next time the heat of anger surfaced, I was determined to allow my breath simply to take the heat to my heart, where I would eventually know how to express it. Moe shared that she had learned anger is energy in motion. It is what we do with the anger that matters.

On the airplane flying back to Scottsdale, I closed my eyes and felt the gratitude of knowing that healing takes its own tender time. I needed to practice going to the silent place and letting go. Tears streamed down my cheeks, and the older woman sitting next to me handed me a tissue. I felt her compassion and thanked her.

It wasn't long until this woman started telling me about her troubled daughter. As she spoke, I listened. I knew the power of story and of being present for her. She spoke for a long time, releasing her anger. She was furious with her daughter. As I listened, I practiced quietly breathing in and out and staying present with her. When we parted, I thanked her for sharing and told her I would hold her and her daughter deep in my heart. I understood and accepted her anger. She gently touched my arm and thanked me.

Walking away, I was aware that I had deeply listened to her. My mind hadn't wandered. I had been present for her. I was so grateful. I was also aware that someone else might have given her advice, but that wasn't me that day. My gift had been to give her my loving heart through compassionate, deep listening.

Part III: Finding Purpose

Purpose and Meaning

SO MUCH WAS GETTING BETTER. I RECONNECTED WITH FAM-
ily and friends and was smiling again. Many of them had been
far more concerned about me than I knew. It was surprising to
learn their concern had extended beyond my divorce. They had
felt the result of what was referred to as my "obsession with *him*
years." I avoided talking very much about what had happened
and instead focused on catching up with the details of what was
happening in their lives. While on the tour, I hadn't paid attention to what was beginning to hold more and more meaning for
me now—the simple joy of relationships. While I had phoned and
seen my parents occasionally, I knew when we were together I
had been preoccupied with my own life. I had never been relaxed
and present with them.

However, a new worry was beginning to move in like a fast
train. I was waking up in the early morning hours wondering
what was next. What was my life purpose? I had learned so much

about the consequences of my insecurities, need to control, fear of not being loved and not paying attention to my own heart. But what was next?

As a young girl, I had gone to church with my family, but religion never got into my bones and soul. We went to a Baptist church every Sunday while I was living at home. Jenny and I didn't listen to the preacher, though. Instead we passed notes about what food we were going to get at Morrison's Cafeteria after church. We loved the fried chicken with okra and Jell-O on the side. I did believe that Jesus loved me because the Bible said so. I also believed that if I wasn't perfect, I would burn in hell.

Years passed, and I no longer believed I would go to hell if I was bad. I also didn't believe religion would give me inner peace. I believed inner peace was within each of us, and it needed to be expressed and let out. With all my heart I wanted this peace. I wanted a meaningful life.

I wanted to know how to find this peace, so I went to workshops and took online seminars. One day I heard a woman say that nothing is more fun than searching for your life purpose. I wasn't in a place to say it was fun, but I loved hearing and reading the stories about how people found their life purposes.

One person said he walked on coals. Afterward, everything became clear to him. Other people talked about their pilgrimages to sacred places, fasting for days, trying out religions different from the one in which they were raised. Still others quit their secure jobs to live in back-to-earth spiritual communities or to volunteer on a mission project. Many of the people I met were vegetarian or vegan. They were taking yoga or tai chi, going to an acupuncturist, drinking herbal teas, buying dream-catchers and Tibetan singing bowls, wearing mala beads, and reading books that had *purpose* and *soul* in the titles. I wasn't alone in my search.

I was introduced to Aura Soma Oils in Sedona, Arizona. Depending upon the color of the oils I chose, a practitioner promised to reveal my mission and soul purpose in this life. I also had tarot card readings and heard the theory that each human being has an inner light that can be nurtured by treatments like Reiki, therapeutic touch, and cranial sacrum massage, as well as by practicing mindfulness and contemplative prayer. People told me how crystals have power; how we all have lives that can be seen in past life regressions; how energy centers in our bodies, known as chakras, need to be balanced. I was given a dream catcher to hang in my room, sage to smudge out evil spirits, and chant CDs to soothe my heart.

Once I entered this world called the New Age, I was startled that there were so many paths to explore. I met truly loving, gentle, sincere people on this journey, but was aware that most of their offerings brought me no closer to know about my life purpose. They didn't fit me.

Moe welcomed all spiritual and religious paths. She encouraged me to seek answers about the deeper meaning of my life *within myself.* She offered guidance mostly in the form of stories, questions, and sharing what she had come to know.

I wanted to be grounded in my own truth and knowing within. But it was easier to have other people tell me about me and my life purpose than to do my own work. Fortunately, the inner work that I had done in CODA and with Moe kept me from accepting that anyone knew more about me than I knew about myself.

I did, however, find asking others very helpful when I looked for an opening to discover the stories of how they had arrived where they were. For example, if they said the color in the oils I chose were telling me that I would most likely be happy in a particular profession, I listened. Then I asked how they had come to know about these oils and learn to read them. I discovered much from their stories, which is in part why I am sharing mine with you.

I could write an entire book about the people and places I explored. What's most important to me is to share how helpful it was to learn the many different ways people choose to express themselves in the world. Wherever I went, though most of the modalities were different from what I chose for myself, I felt loving intention. The stories decreased my judgment of others in proportion to the increase of my understanding. My world was widening and deepening.

I asked myself and others if the longing to find a life purpose was universal. I met many people who were trying to create bridges between their higher and lower selves—or, as they often said, between their true selves and their limited, earthly selves. I was definitely not alone in my longing and quest.

Where had I been for so long to have missed out on all of this? While on the tour, were others also thinking about this? He had found his life purpose naturally. No wonder he wanted me to live mine.

Deepening

ONE SUMMER DAY, I WAS LISTENING TO AN AUDIO TAPE AS I drove. I heard the person on the tape say, "Inner peace is closer than breathing, nearer than our hands and feet."

I pulled my car off to the side of the road as the sun was setting in the Arizona sky. I turned off the audio. As I gazed at the sun making her way down, I felt an overwhelming sense of gratitude for my journey to that point. I was grateful to feel, not think, that inner peace was closer than my breathing and nearer than my hands and feet. It reminded me to know, not only believe, that inner peace was already within me. It was in a place where I could surrender to a higher power without any proof. I was letting go with each in-and-out breath, letting go each time I chose love over fear, and letting go when I allowed thoughts of the past to pass by rather than attaching myself to them.

At about this time, I was given a poem written by Rev. Safire Rose that to this day means a lot to me.

She Let Go

She let go. Without a thought or a word, she let go.
She let go of fear. She let go of the judgments.
She let go of the confluence of opinions
swarming around her head.
She let go of the committee of indecision within her.
She let go of all the 'right' reasons. Wholly and completely,
without hesitation or worry, she just let go.
She didn't ask anyone for advice. She didn't read a
book on how to let go ... She didn't search the scriptures.

She just let go.
She let go of all of the memories that held her back.
She let go of all of the anxiety that kept
her from moving forward.
She let go of the planning and all of the
calculations about how to do it just right.
She didn't promise to let go.
She didn't journal about it.
She didn't write the projected date in her day-timer.
She made no public announcement and put no ad in the paper.
She didn't check the weather report or read her daily horoscope.
She just let go.
She didn't analyze whether she should let go.
She didn't call her friends to discuss the matter.
She didn't do a five-step Spiritual Mind Treatment.
She didn't call the prayer line.
She didn't utter one word. She just let go.
No one was around when it happened.
There was no applause or congratulations.
No one thanked her or praised her.

No one noticed a thing.
Like a leaf falling from a tree, she just let go.
There was no effort. There was no struggle.
It wasn't good and it wasn't bad.
It was what it was, and it is just that.
In the space of letting go, she let it all be.
A small smile came over her face.
A light breeze blew through her.
And the sun and the moon shone forevermore.

I shared with Moe that I was sort of getting it, but the moments were fleeting and I wanted the moments to link together. Sitting at the round table, she said she loved my desire to want to continue to *meet myself* through my search. She offered that it was the continual meeting of herself through all of her experiences that had led her to knowing her truth.

While I don't remember her words exactly, this is what I do remember her saying: "Jocelyn, consider that like many other people today, you are waking up from a very deep sleep. It seems each of us awakens in our own way from the separation from God that we created through our human personalities, struggles, and challenges. What I have learned to be foundational is that you are sincerely exhibiting the qualities of a woman who was once lost, and is now waking up from the illusion that you needed to please others in order for them to love you; from not knowing who you are and what's right for you; and from believing that the material world and status would make you happy."

Her words penetrated. I actually *felt* my sincerity and passion to be whole. This wasn't only her truth; it was mine too.

In the Sufi wisdom tradition, is it said that either we are walking away from God, we are walking toward God, or we were with God all along. I loved the clarity of this and knew I wanted to walk with God. Joyful tears rolled down my cheeks as I stood up from the table and said I was going to be with nature.

As I walked the path among the trees, I heard the familiar roar of horses running across the meadow next to Moe's. I paused. I listened. I breathed deeply. I remembered the teachings I had so diligently been working on. I stayed present to my feelings and to the moment. My heart beat faster and faster. I was keeping pace with the cantering of the horses. Recognizing this familiar rhythm, I felt a distant invitation to return to the one place I had felt so alive as a young girl—my horses. As the invitation made its way into my conscious awareness, I felt what I can only describe as moments when I touched the blazing fire of inner peace. Something beyond me was pulsating within me, and my mind released from striving to define my search for my life purpose.

The More

MY LIFE MOVED QUICKLY AFTER THOSE MOMENTS. MY heart had awakened. I knew there was more to me than my mind. Whether one called it God or Spirit or Higher Power made no difference to me, but I heard the call and experienced "the More." I knew the horses were calling me back to a time in my life when the wind touched my cheeks, and I felt more love and purpose than I had since known in my life.

I slowly walked back inside to sit down at the round wooden table, where I could see the trees through the bay window. I fumbled for words as I tried to share my experience. Moe encouraged me to take my time. She said, "We have lots of time. Just share what you want and can." I slowly shared that to live life only for the satisfaction of emotional pleasures, material security, and personal ambition wasn't enough for me.

Hearing myself say this, once again I made my way to an inner area where the undergrowth of the forest had been cleared and rays of sun were streaming through the leaves. I sat down, took a deep belly breath, and asked about my longing for more. I wrote in my journal, "I want to know how I can add more love in the world."

Sitting in this beautiful space with the trees, I was aware of how I was noticing the beauty of the textured bark, the smell of the rich dirt, the sprawl of leaf ferns leaning toward the light, and the wonder of the natural world.

My deep belly breathing had been difficult at first, but gradually it was becoming more natural for me. I whispered out loud, "Thank you." The gratitude I felt for knowing there was an offering that I could give to the world was immense.

Much of what I had read and learned on my journey to this point was making more sense. Many people have written or spoken about the higher self within. Finally, I was beginning to understand and have a relationship with that part of me. I was learning how worldly influences and my need to be loved had crystallized into a mask that I could have worn all of my life. I had heard somewhere that if you wear a mask too long, it will become your face.

Had he not been true to what he needed for himself, I might have remained in my false self forever.

I heard a story about the difference between heaven and hell. In summary, hell was depicted as a place where people sat in misery in front of extraordinary foods, using spoons so long they could never reach their mouths. People in heaven sat in front of the same extraordinary foods with the same long spoons—and happily fed each other. I was very moved by this story. In my heart, I knew all these spiritual paths I was exploring ultimately said that happiness, contentment, and inner peace required acts of compassion, helping each other remember the divine light or presence within each of us.

I was beginning to feel compassion for myself. I don't think I had ever felt this before. For much of my life I had been responding to life in fear. I wanted to be a person who would take the long spoon to feed someone else and to allow someone to feed me. I wanted to feel compassion for everyone. I didn't want to try to be compassionate—I wanted to feel it. I wanted it to be a natural state for me, all the time, no matter what.

I have reflected on the images of this story many times. It has called me back to who I really want to be.

Unconditional Love

My parents said that I was born wanting a horse, and that much of my childhood centered on doing whatever it took to be near horses—riding horses, owning horses, participating in competitions, and eventually talking about them. It gave me a special identity to be the one who competed in the elite equestrian world.

I see how my love of horses started out with purity and innocence. The memories of my dad taking my hand and walking with me to a nearby meadow to feed the horses carrots remain cherished images I hold in my heart. The memories of my mom always making sure that I could be with horses fills me with gratitude for her incredible love for me.

When I heard horses running nearby and was transported to the peace beyond my understanding, I once again realized my horses and my whippets have offered me more steady emotional support than I can possibly express. I am aware they have loved and cared for me even when I have been uncaring. They have fed my soul and given me the benefit of the doubt, unconditionally.

During my visits to Moe, I told my story in various ways: sometimes in spontaneous scenes from my life, sometimes in specific narratives such as "A time when I was angry" or "I remember when he told me this." As I shared my stories later with other individuals or groups, I learned to step out and witness the story as if I were witnessing a movie. As I learned to witness the various scenes of my life, I felt more and more kindness, understanding, and compassion for everyone. I saw how hard I had been on myself, as well as how self-centered and judgmental I had been.

Another practice I started at this time was a daily inventory of how I behaved with others, the true intentions behind my actions, and how to sweep my own side of the street. I learned to review my roles and actions in all of my relationships and to take full responsibility for my part in any disharmony. I was learning about powerlessness, unmanageability, and taking my own inventory rather than inventorying others. I was starting to believe unconditional love was possible but required a major shift in my heart and consciousness. Believing that it was now possible felt like a big step.

Yet memories of him still were around every corner, no matter how much work I was doing to make them fade.

Geographic Change

I WANTED A BREAK FROM LIVING IN SCOTTSDALE.

I wanted out of what felt like his world for a while. The intensity of the memories in the house, the questions from people in the restaurants, and the memories of our shared time in the area were tiring. I wanted to scream, "We aren't married anymore, and I don't know where he is!" Of course, I didn't. Instead, I remembered that these people didn't have a clue about our lives. They were just curious. I also remembered there was a time when I had loved it that people knew I was married to him.

I was afraid leaving the area might seem like I was trying to heal through a "geographic cure." Over and over in CODA meetings I heard about people escaping because they thought a new setting would take care of their problems. By now, I had put in intense months of daily work. I knew nothing on the outside was going to change my insides. Yet a change might be what I needed.

I looked forward to being away from everything familiar. I

could tell the inner work I had done up to this point was beginning to manifest in my life. I made a commitment to myself not to google or research anything that had to do with our parting. For eight months, I stayed singularly focused on getting to know me and loving myself again.

Remembering the peace I felt with my animals, I researched how I might help myself and others with horses. It wasn't long before I learned about a program in Kentucky that offered a certification in therapeutic riding instruction. So I signed up for this program and traveled there in the spring of 2011 to learn how to help special needs children have transformative experiences with horses. It was there that I learned a deep sense of compassion for children and the powerful healing nature of horses.

My time in Kentucky was filled with working at the riding center and taking the dogs on long country walks. I loved my time there and will forever cherish the memories of sitting in the lush green grass and letting the sun wash over me like a warm blanket.

I continued to meditate every day. Finally, my mind was thinking less about him. I was grateful that I could feel some inner peace.

Connecting through Blogging

WHILE I WAS WORKING AT THE RIDING CENTER, SEVERAL people asked me about my healing journey. I told them a little of my story. They encouraged me to start blogging because they felt my story might help others.

I had heard of blogging. All I could think of was Carrie Bradshaw on *Sex and the City* and her kind of blogging. So I researched it and one night began my own blog, *From Horses with Love*. The following is an example of a blog post I wrote in 2011:

Trusting the New

"Trusting the New" is an entry incorporating a few concepts and experiences I have shared with you already.

In the blog titled *Authenticity and the Power to Change,* I shared what I have learned about trust in my life with horses, and how I carry that out to become my authentic self. As far as change or "newness" is concerned, I touched on that in previous blog entry, *Stretching My Mind.* Today I would like to mix the two.

Mahatma Gandhi said, "You must be the change you see in the world."

When I think of change, exploring a new world, or even entering a new day, I wonder how would I respond to the situation if I were a horse. I am not going to physically act like a horse, although I think my sister would attest to me acting like one during my younger years.

So how would a horse react to change or something "new"? I didn't realize it until as of late, but I have been witnessing this exact activity for many years. Horses do react to change in their own unique way. For instance, when I took the horses to a horse show they had never been to, they were on high alert. Cordino especially—he was a stallion and the head of the herd at the time. I would approach the new show ground, and immediately all the horses would start to nicker (this is a sound that horses make when they communicate with other herd members). His head would pop out of his trailer stall window. His ears would be straight up, and his eyes looked intently at what was to come. The handsome stallion did not run away, overreact, or become a possum. He did what horses do ... breathe and be present.

It seems to me that being a horse involves many aspects of understanding nature and knowing when to make small adjustments when new areas of its life are revealed. This is a beautiful act to observe in the wild. The most subtle flick of the ear (awareness), swish of the tail, or foot replacement is all it takes. I understand that their ability to be present in every moment is what keeps them growing and changing into their forever evolving spirit and selves.

A friend said to me the other day, "I think some horses are just brain dead."

I shook my head and said, "Really? Where did you learn that?"

She was stunned that I did not agree with her.

I know for a fact that all horses are extremely intelligent beings. They are here to show me a lot about who I am.

The horse in the photo above is Sirocco Van Heppershoff. My gentle Belgian gelding is now the partner to a young lady named Kelsey. Sirocco was an amazing teacher for me because he showed up different every day. He was brought to me as a messenger, to give me many lessons about how to create change and how to just go with "it."

I honor the horse as my teacher. I have nothing but gratitude for the way horses have shown me to accept and trust change and the "new" with dignity. So when I am introduced to something new, I have an image in my mind of how I will respond. I know I have a herd, a community, love, and, most of all, trust in myself to back me up.

This is perhaps a new way for some people to view horses. For me, I see them as my guide. I could go as far as saying they are my oracle. I believe they are the way to learn, discover, and reveal how to trust the new. The new brings life to my soul, and it is a part of being a human being.

This blog has taken me on a discovery of self-awareness and insight into my life that I did not expect. I am blessed to have so many wonderful friends and family as my support and inspiration. I have to thank the horses because without them, I don't think I would be who I am today.

Love, Jocelyn

It felt good to have my own little space to share my voice and vision for deeper relationships with the equine world. I remember sitting at the dining room table I had purchased at IKEA and logging onto Blogger, a free blog platform. In fifteen minutes I had a blog and had posted my first entry, called "My Corso V." You may remember Corso from earlier in the book; he was the first horse he and I purchased, and to this day Corso remains in my heart.

I blogged every day, and soon the blog became a place many people went to for inspiration and to know a little more about me. It felt good to share parts of my story. I was beginning to hear my own voice. I found blogging a wonderful way for me to express my inner life.

In November of 2011, my internship was complete in Kentucky, it was time to return to Arizona. The divorce was final, and I was moving back into Fanfol, the dream house we had shared as a married couple. As I drove into the area, I remembered how I had thought we were going to be so happy here and how excited I had been to apply my interior design skills and create a home, not just a house.

As I drove into the driveway, everything looked different to me. Many of our material possessions were gone. I knew to touch the memories and feelings lightly—not bypass them, but also not dwell on them. I had done too much work to allow myself to fall backward.

I redesigned and restyled the house for the dogs and me. I added more color, brought in more vintage pieces, and lived like it was my own house and not one I shared with him.

Within a few weeks, I felt comfortable and began riding again to inspire me as to what my next adventure would be. Being with the horses allowed my mind to stay soft, open to my inner voice, so I could clearly hear it and it could guide me about what I was to do. The horses were once again an outside refuge; I could spend all day at the barn and not say a word to anyone. I often took the dogs and set them up on a blanket in the office, where they would sleep while I brushed all the horses.

As I rode around the arena, I not only watched myself, but I heard other girls criticizing themselves for not being perfect.

I saw their tears. If they didn't get the distance to a jump just right, they said harsh, negative things about themselves and their horses. I remembered when I used to do the same thing. I could identify with the emotional pain of thinking a slight error was the end of the world. Fortunately, by now I had come to know the pain was their teacher. It was theirs and no longer mine. My nature is always to help, and I knew interfering would not truly *help* them; it would only hinder their process.

I realized anxiety played a big role in the competitive horse world, and my next business and blog were born. I began a blog, *Jocelyn Casey Performance Coaching* as a way to share my stories and help others who suffered from anxiety when it came to competition. I shared many of the same tools I had been learning in equestrian language. No one caught on to the concept, but I knew I was a bit early in bringing this to the world of competitors, who often blamed the horses and themselves for not performing perfectly. The idea of progress, not perfection, had not yet penetrated this world.

The following is a blog entry I wrote at this time:

> I remember the day my trainer let me ride Colina—a young bay Holsteiner mare who stood just fifteen hands tall. Her eyes were soft and kind, her heart was brave and feminine. Knowing she had only recently entered the earthly realm, I paused under the big sky in reverence for her beginning of life. In the pause, I wondered what her earthly journey was going to be like. My mind traveled to faraway places, and I mentally "wrote" a story about Colina's life. As I fantasized about her future, I gradually lost awareness of my body and of staying in the present moment.

I have been told we "get off the path at times so we can remember what it looks like to be on the path," but apparently I needed to experience it. When I lost track of the present moment, I forgot Colina needed a little hand-holding. I forgot she was very young and excited about life. I forgot we would need to practice boundaries and develop a cadence together. I forgot to tune in to her disposition and individual mannerisms. Simply, I was "out of my body," and my mind was far away from our connection.

The sun was shining. It was a beautiful day. The shadows of human arms and legs were especially visible to a horse's eye. Very visible. In fact, Colina could so clearly see the shadows, she decided that if she jumped sideways, we could miss the shadows! Needless to say she caught me by surprise. I went one way, she went the other, and I fell to the ground.

With dirt in my ears, eyes, nails, and scratches on my back, I was jolted back into reality. In a flash, I saw how I had not been paying attention, and I felt tremendous gratitude for Colina helping me to remember what often happens when we "drift away" from what we are doing. I felt fortunate for the jolt and even though it was a tough fall, it could have been much worse. I looked into her eyes with true gratitude.

Fortunately, Colina did not run away frightened. I suspect this was the first time someone had fallen off of her. Instead, she looked at me as if to say, "Ummm ... *thank you for not blaming me.*" *I remembered so many times when I was not able to take responsibility for my part when there was disharmony* between me and my horse. I could not punish my brave mare for my forgetting to be present. Most of all, I could thank her for helping me remember what happens when we fall off the path.

Thank you, Colina ... *with love, Jocelyn*

My adventure continued when I moved to Germany in May of 2012 to train with an internationally esteemed trainer from Denmark. I was going to use my experience to help others and, at the same time, learn more. I learned many new, wonderful skills. As I listened to the trainers and sat in the silence of the deep breath, more parts of me surfaced.

It took about a year before my desire for interior design and creating peaceful spaces returned. It was as if my soul were retrieving the passions that had been dismantled when I was focused on him and traveling in the golf world. I hadn't forgotten that I had wanted a professional career in interior design. I remembered the successes I had already had in the field. But I didn't feel the call to it again until I was working with the trainers. They were so focused and disciplined with every move that in many ways it was like watching professional golfers at a tournament.

I am convinced that the Denmark trainer's ability to focus was contagious and my inner focus increased. Perhaps this was one of the reasons for me to be around people who had something I wanted. I wanted to travel deeper for the focus and inner peace that I felt around them. Once again, conscious deep breathing helped to clear my mind.

Over time, I developed a longing to design and style my own home. I began a blog called *The Little Room of Style* in April 2013. There, I shared my inspirations for interior design, style, entertaining, and traveling. I embraced my skills for creating interiors and styling homes. I practiced photography every single day and would often stay up all night editing images.

When I began blogging on this site I was obsessed with every aspect of the blog and wanted it to appear excellent; perfectionism still loomed. I would often spend thirteen hours working on a post! I had become more involved in the inner design of my life and wanted to share it with others. Many things came up for me while I was living in another country: language, connection, communication, and general relationship challenges.

The following is from *The Little Room of Style* in April 2013:

> Creating a meaningful life used to mean something quite different to me many years ago. Today, I crave a deep and meaningful experience here on earth. Without thinking about it too much, I took notice of the things that made my day significant. I have come to know now that these things come naturally when I am centered and aligned. Staying connected to my source is a moment-to-moment practice. I am going to share with you a few ways I create meaning in my life each and every day. I hope some of these little things will spark you to extend even more goodness into your life and the lives of others today.
>
> 1. *Connect.* Each morning before my feet hit the ground, I connect with myself through the powers that are greater than me. I set my

intentions, which sometimes look a little different each day. Today my intention was to stay balanced, no matter what.

2. *Read inspiring material.* I know my mind is most open first thing in the morning, so I make sure to read material that will move me forward and inspire me for the day. For example, I read a book called *The Book of Awakening* by Mark Nepo. I also love to visit the Facebook page of Earthschool Harmony for its sweet photos and quotes. The same goes for music; the vibration in music can alter your inner balance immensely. If I am feeling a little somber, I put on some Beyoncé. If I need to steady my mind, I listen to Ambient Radio on Pandora.

3. *Listen.* Support a friend or family member by simply listening to them, *deeply.* I find when I truly listen to someone's story, we both feel better. Do you ever notice how many times you are interrupted while telling a story? Just by listening to the words of someone you meet, you can provide meaning to both of you. Listening is also learning. Being heard is healing.

4. *Respond.* For me, replying to comments on my blog is a principle I live by. If a reader takes the time to comment, you bet your bottom dollar I will make the time to respond genuinely. It is my belief everyone appreciates a response.

5. *Take a walk and smile.* It is often referred to as "free therapy," but smiling is something of a wonder to me. Do you ever notice how you feel when someone smiles at you, especially a stranger? Your spirits are suddenly lifted a tad, right? I must admit, there are times when I don't feel like smiling. When this happens, I encourage myself to get outside, walk in the park, and find something beautiful to smile at.

6. *Become a mentor.* I believe we don't have to seek out others to mentor; we patiently wait for them to come to us. I mentor a young photographer in Florida, and our relationship creates meaning in my life like no other. My assignment with her is mainly to encourage her and provide her with support. In turn, I become a better person and so does she. We learn through one another, and this is a true gift.

7. *Give thanks.* A sincere thank-you goes a long way in terms of meaning. I think the act of giving thanks is somewhat watered down. So many times (before) I would thank someone and not even look him or her in the eye. Today, I make a conscious effort to look the cashier or salesperson in the eye and kindly say, "Thank *you*." I find most people are flattered or stunned, but the main point is I acted upon my principles for life.

8. *Create a manifesto or principles for the way you choose to live your life.* I will say that the moment I created my manifesto, my life changed. When I was unclear or too quick to respond to something or someone, I would remind myself of my principles for life. My decision would become crystal clear. My manifesto looks a little something like this list, but you can do it any way you wish.

9. *Align the mind and body.* Meditation can look different for each person, depending on his or her practice. For me, I practice a walking meditation as well as Transcendental Meditation (TM). TM involves using a mantra that is given to you by your teacher or instructor. Meditating allows me to stay connected to my source and stay aligned throughout the day so I can create a deep and meaningful life.

10. *Create a mantra.* My life would not be the same if I did not have my mantras. I have some that were given to me by my teacher and are sacred to me. I have some that I share with others. For me, repeating my mantra creates balance and alignment in my mind and body. This keeps me fresh and revitalized all day. Mostly, it keeps me out of my head, which can sometimes become cluttered with thoughts and opinions.

I remembered how the power of story profoundly helped me, so in my blogs I shared more and more of what I was learning in

Germany and my travels in Europe. As these parts of me revealed themselves, I felt excited about life again. I wanted to share more intimate details of my life, and that was reflected in a shift in my blog. I removed all categories from *The Little Room of Style* except for the life piece and only shared the more sacred parts of my journey. I also began publishing *The Inner Interior*, a blog dedicated to the art of mindful living. The feeling of being at home washed over me again and again. I understood now that the journey was long, and with time, my vision became clearer. I have no doubt this may evolve and transition into something new. When that day comes, I will embrace it as I did my other projects.

I love sharing all these different ways of expression. At one time in my life I heard someone criticized for doing a little of this and a little of that, suggesting she was all over the place. I shared this with Moe and she invested me with the credentials she loves to share: Jocelyn Hefner, DLOCS—Does Lots Of Cool Stuff. She reminded me that of course I have been all over place. It's wonderful to travel into so many different aspects of life. Yes, I have had the money to do this, and I am grateful. However, DLOCS credentials don't require money; they require passion, creativity, courage, and a desire to be fully alive and not stay stuck.

As I continued to learn about the many different aspects within me, Moe suggested that we all come to this world with traits that are uniquely our own. I came to understand how an aspect of me had become a character chameleon to fill my need to be loved, accepted, and admired. I was also learning that my true self was growing. Now I wanted my own relationship with God.

I heard a lot about connecting with God through spiritual practice: prayer, meditation, deep breathing, visualizations, vision quests, sacred dancing, music, art, sacred readings, and chanting. I am sure there are many other ways, but these were the ones I was reading about and experiencing.

As I ventured through many of these practices, I was very grateful to have someone with whom to discuss what was happening to me. I had learned so much and was feeling more peace than I had ever felt in my life. However, worldly thoughts always seemed to loom in the background.

Sometimes I felt like two very distinct people. One person was frantically dealing with everyday issues: money, health insurance, the house, the pups, irritation, frustration, and the mental traffic of life. The other person was immersed in the search for a loving, peace- filled, conscious life. I wanted the peace more of the time. I wanted it all the time, but I didn't know if that was possible.

When I shared these thoughts with Moe, once again I was met with assurance that my desire was part of the journey toward unification of my two selves. I shared that sometimes God felt far away and wasn't an active part of my everyday life. Both my sincerity and frustration were noted, and Moe shared another story that had been told to her.

> A long time ago there was a community of people who had a very big problem in their village. The problem was so big they were willing to go all over the world trying to find the answer, the solution. Day after day, month after month, year after year, they all lived in great quandary as to how to handle this problem.

> One warm day, one of the community members walked down the path near their village and sat on a rock. He was just sitting on the rock, eating an artichoke, feeling great gratitude for his life. He was not thinking about his community's problem

for a change; he was not seeking any answers. He was simply sitting on the rock, eating his artichoke in a state of gratitude for the beauty around him, for the warmth of the sun, the wonderful taste of the artichoke.

It wasn't long until, in this restful, open, grateful state, he felt warmth surround his entire body. He felt connected to everything around him and a sense of peace that was beyond his understanding. Out of nowhere and everywhere, he "heard" the answer to the question that the community had been asking for all those years; he got the solution.

Of course, he was thrilled and quickly ran back to the village and gathered everyone around him. He told them he had the answer, the solution. Immediately, they did exactly what he told them to do, and the problem was solved. Everyone was leaping with joy and wondered how did he find the answer? Wanting to share, the man simply told them he had walked the forest path, was sitting on a rock eating an artichoke, feeling the blessedness of life, when all

of a sudden he felt this warmth and the "answer" came to him.

Listening attentively, the villagers said, almost in unison, "Where's the rock? What kind of artichoke?"

After Moe shared this story, she suggested I take time to re-flect on what it meant to me. So I did. It didn't take long for me to realize I was looking for the one rock and the right artichoke to connect with God. When I shared this, Moe invited me to "take one seat in the room"—a term she uses to describe herself when she stopped seeking God. It was clear I had been doing a little of this and a little of that, focusing more on the rock and the artichoke than being present and listening within. I had been seeking, and it was time to face my resistance to meditation.

I was still scared of being quiet for very long. I also knew that creating an authentic spiritual life required true contem-plation—a sincere ability to listen to how God speaks through and to me.

One Seat in the Room

I HAVEN'T TOLD YOU YET ABOUT MY EXPOSURE TO WHAT seemed like a million different ways to meditate: Transcendental Meditation, Mindfulness Meditation, Tonglen Meditation, Vipissana (Insight Meditation), Counting Meditation, Mantra Meditation, Walking Meditation, the Jesus Prayer ... on and on. I started with various dynamic, moving meditations. I emptied out thoughts. But I had not yet practiced a silent, deeper meditation. I was afraid I couldn't sit quietly for a long time.

I quickly learned there is no one way suitable for all people. Every person must ultimately find the way that is right for them. For me, meditation calls forth a deep sense of humility and letting go of personal selfhood.

Many meditation teachers and books reminded me that meditation is not easy—simple, but not easy. I was aware I was trying many different types of meditation because nothing was quite enough for me. Was anything ever going to be enough for me?

It was suggested that I listen to and read true stories from others who had found the meditation practice that was best for them. I welcomed the idea and trusted I would hear something that would help me, and I did. I had the opportunity to absorb many different stories in different ways and was so grateful that I could finally feel what was right for me. Being able to identify and feel my feelings via deep breathing was one of the most important aspects of my journey to this point, but of course there were miles to go.

I spent many months exploring how others found and developed their meditation practices. I welcomed meeting more people who felt like I was beginning to feel. Inner peace required a paradigm shift in consciousness, in how I saw the world. All my experiences were lessons to help me learn and develop a new perspective on life. For example, I could see him as a victimizer, and I could be a victim of divorce, or I could see him as a teacher who helped wake me up to the fear that was permeating my life.

My gratitude for life was increasing, my compassion for others was expanding, and my desire to be authentic and real in every interaction was burning in my heart. I was slowly assimilating and discerning my truth.

The common thread in all that I was listening to and reading was that if I kept myself unreasonably busy—as I had most of my life—and did not turn within frequently throughout the day, I would not have access to my higher self, my inner wisdom, or the still, small voice within me that never left. Over and over again, in different ways, I heard, "There is a presence that dwells within us; to connect with this presence, we must go to the silence."

I began, again, with a vow to sit in silence every morning. I had said previously that I would do this but found that many days I rushed off into the world. I liked the idea of making a vow. Somehow the word "vow" brought a feeling of sacred seriousness to this practice. I said my vow alone in nature. It wasn't dramatic; it was real. I loved being so clear and out loud about my intent.

I decided to try Mantra Meditation in addition to following my breath. I think I was drawn to it because someone once joked that my mantra had been "Him, Him, Him" for many years, and I was ready for a redo. I learned the Sanskrit word *mantra* is a blending of many words that ultimately mean protector, mind, and sound. Apparently Gandhi repeated "Ram" (God) throughout the day as his mantra for many, many years. An assassin shot and killed him. The story goes that as he was falling to the ground he said, "Jai Ram" (Hail God). This story helped me to see how mantra practice could train my mind in what was beginning to feel like the right direction for me.

Moe was friends with Bo and Sita Lozoff, who founded, along with Ram Dass, the Human Kindness Organization. Mo shared that when she was blind, her mantra was given to her by Bo Lozoff: "Happy with sight; happy without sight." It was not surprising that she received the Happy Patient Award at the University of Illinois Retina Department in 2008.

Bo and Sita dedicated their lives to helping people in prison create sacred lives in the prison community. They offer several mantra phrases that I love:

It's good to be alive.

Happy with, happy without, no matter what.

Peace, be still.

I can do hard.

Whatever happens to one person can happen to me.

I chose one mantra and vowed to say it within throughout the day. In the morning, I anchored it by saying it out loud over and over again until I was whispering it. Then I allowed it to run inside me like a waterfall for a few minutes. I also made sticky notes and put them everywhere to remind me. It was hard, but as

Bo and Sita Lozoff said to prisoners, "You can do hard." I wanted to stick with it. I can honestly say it was the first time in my life that I stayed with a spiritual practice.

After thirty days, it began to call me. I tried different mantras. I loved it. My mind felt more tethered to my heart. It was much easier for me to focus and concentrate. I knew I was a humble beginner and that without daily practice, my mind could easily wander the globe again and run storylines.

I was cautioned not to share my mantra. A spiritual practice is like planting a sacred seed in the earth; the seed will grow on its own with natural sunlight and water. If we dig into the soil to see if the seed is growing, we will damage its roots. By talking about it, I was likely to engage my mind, which was the opposite of what I wanted.

Eventually, my mind was not constantly chattering, and I found it easier to pull back from the chaos of life. I was more aware of all of my thoughts in the day, my actions, my feelings, and my relationships. I watched how I behaved rather how others behaved.

After several years of daily meditation, I have come to know there is no best or right way to meditate. It is individual and personal. What has remained constant for me is knowing I have a place of refuge within me now, and it is a soft place. I don't have to keep searching on the outside for inner peace and a relationship with God. It may elude me at times, but I know it's there. I know if I let too much worldly information feed my mind, I will most likely return to my codependent thinking and actions.

I am grateful that I learned not to make a big deal about how to sit, where to sit, or how long to meditate. I prefer to meditate alone. I allow my breath to direct me. One time I was inwardly directed to light a candle and simply focus on the flame. Countless thoughts floated by, but I tried to let them pass. (Sometimes I do engage them, and it's always a disaster.) Several years later, I read that this was an acknowledged meditation practice called "focusing on the flame." I was hearing the whisper—only this time, it wasn't about fear.

All of this guidance led me within, to the soft place of the heart where inner wisdom awaits. Moe often said, "Where love meets love, healing begins." At first I didn't grasp this, but the deep meaning has been revealed to me. When Moe's eyesight in one eye returned, she shared that the doctors loved her and she loved them. In surgery, she knew love was coming through the doctors in the surgical procedures, and she was in a state of love, not fear, to receive their love. Healing happened. While I can't explain this, I do understand it.

In the beginning, I could not say, "Happy with him; happy without him," because I wasn't. However, I deepened in a daily spiritual practice with spiritual principles. Today I can say this about any him or her. My happiness is no longer dependent on an outside source—although people sure can contribute to my happiness.

Moe repeatedly refused to be my source. She was simply one of the guides to my inner source. I was so vulnerable when I met her; I am sure it would have been easy for me to become dependent on her. I am grateful that she always encouraged me to check with my own wisdom. Sometimes I disagreed with her, and she loved it and always listened to what I had to say. Moe modeled being a person with opinions, judgments, preferences, and definition, not a person who was judgmental or opinionated. This modeling has meant more to me than I can ever express.

Gradually, I learned that my life purpose was not to be an interior designer or an equestrian instructor or the spouse of a professional golfer. Today, it is my heart's desire to give and receive love in every interaction, no matter how anyone else behaves. This has required a form of mental surgery to cut away my desire for any person, place, thing, circumstance, or condition to give me sustaining happiness or be different from what they already are.

It has been with meditation that my heart has expanded to include all different ways to find God. In the silence, I touch the presence of love, and I want to radiate this love. Throughout the day I return to the silence, sometimes for a second. Sometimes I see a bathroom as my temple, where I can go and breathe deeply and return to the truth that I know rather than what has been told to me in the marketplace of ideas and consumerism.

When I am listening to someone, I have learned to stay tethered to my heart by breathing deeply. I am not perfect at this; I can forget, but I no longer require perfection. I know that if I do not start my day with meditation and the spiritual principles that resonate for me, my personality can quickly take over. It isn't long before I am self-conscious rather than love conscious.

Through meditation, it was imparted that my foremost task is to fill my consciousness with love, forgiveness, gratitude, loyalty, and devotion to the sacredness of life and God. I see my role in life as to think less about me and more about how I can be a transparency for love. I have found one body of spiritual teaching that I read daily. I carry the principles offered in the teachings of Jesus throughout my day, quietly and confidently.

The Journey Continues

ON OCTOBER 13, 2014, I MARRIED ANOTHER WONDERFUL man, and on December 14, 2014, our son Oskar was born. It is our deepest desire to raise our child with conscious awareness and to participate in helping all of our children fall in love with life.

When I started my inner journey, I longed for meaning. The shoes, handbags, butlers, drivers, and private planes were not doing it for me anymore. I wanted more substance in my life, and I asked for it. What I didn't know was that my four-year journey would lead me to truly live a meaningful life. At the end of the day, living a life of meaning begins with kindness. I am learning my new definition of that word every single day.

In Closing

In one of my meetings with Moe, as we sat around the fire, we talked about what inner peace means. She shared, and I remembered from my childhood, "My peace, I give unto you: not as the world giveth, give I unto you" (John 14:27 KJV).

Moe suggested I spend time reflecting on this for thirty days, as a practice. I took the challenge, and it was revealed to me that as long as I looked to people and circumstances for peace, I wouldn't find it. I began to experience "my peace" as a gentle spirit that wells up within me and has no relationship to the state of affairs in my life—although ultimately it resolves all of my affairs. It was powerful for me to reflect on this one saying for a month.

My needs, my wants, paled when I remembered that my sufficiency is in the Infinite Invisible. Moe shared that she knew this to be practicing the presence of God. The Hebrews called it keeping the mind stayed on God and acknowledging God in all ways. Jesus called it abiding in the Word.

As I said in the beginning, I am grateful, despite the heart-aches, for the journey I have shared here. Many of us awaken through failed relationships, or through loss of money, power, and health, or through drugs … the list goes on and on. Some of us die in these openings. Some of us remain victims. Some of us experience a shift in how we see the world and our relationship to it.

While I have much to learn, I have come to see that the key to my happiness has been learning to let go of how I think things should be. I embrace how they are. I have learned to speak my truth, care for people rather than take care of them, and know we are all "walking each other home." Over and over again on my journey, many people said that in order to find peace, they had to surrender their definition of peace. At first this was difficult for me to grasp, but as I surrendered and starting seeing life as an evolving journey of spiritual growth, I looked for the lessons in my challenges. I have come to believe that everything happens for reason, and there is no such thing as failure.

It was in my search for God that I learned I was seeking freedom from my limited mind being the master and trying to control the outcomes of life. As I write this, I feel so inadequate in expressing this knowing, but perhaps in your journey you have discovered this as well. It feels radically different from the way I was taught. To receive guidance and insights from beyond my mind has changed … everything.

I love this:

> Of all that God has shown me
> I can speak just the smallest word,
> Not more than a honey bee
> Takes on his foot
> From an over-spilling jar.
> —Mechtild of Magdeburg

In the pause, in my deep breathing, in silence, in sacred readings, I am learning about following this inner guidance rather than my ego mind. My ego mind was completely in charge until it couldn't be. His leaving opened the door to my surrendering to my higher power. This surrender propelled my learning to act from a different place with different intentions. I had indeed veered from my innate connection with God. I was seeking recognition, approval, respect, and fortune.

Today, my path is one of wanting to live by universal principles of kindness and generosity to myself and all of life. Wayne Dyer said it well in one of his workshops I attended online: "When you change the way you look at things, the things you look at change."

This shift in consciousness has required a new lifestyle. I have learned new habits, such as not touching the floor in the morning until I have made my conscious connection with God. I have learned to slow down and breathe when someone else is talking, so I can hear that person and my inner guidance. I know that when I wake up, if I immediately connect with the outside world of ideas, such as Facebook, I will be on my way to my ego mind running me versus the spiritual principles that I want to live by. I am constantly amazed at how quickly my ego mind can be engaged if I do not stay tethered to my heart.

Today, if I were asked to recommend one essential practice, it would be to meditate. As I have said, there are many different ways, but meditation develops focused attention and awareness. I am happy to join with many people who also believe meditation is foundational to a spiritual life. I am happy that I did not get attached to a specific type of meditation. I don't need to meditate for twenty minutes or sit in a certain way. I know it is different for each of us. If we want to learn, we will be guided to the best place for our individual natures.

I believe we all need to look to the silent awareness within to connect with our truth. In the silence, I have learned to bypass the mind and access my true nature. When I don't go to the silence and make the connection, all the behaviors and thought patterns that I expressed while traveling the tour are waiting to take over again.

Severing the thought forms that connected me to my past way of thinking has taken far more work than I ever dreamed. Fortunately, my parents always modeled persistence. I see now that it doesn't matter if I have enough willpower or intelligence. What matters is persistence. I have come to believe that spiritual inquiry only started with my longing to know who I truly am. My revelations haven't been mental; they have been visceral. I often feel warmth, like an internal spark, that reminds me of my essential nature beyond the constriction of my ego mind. As I have grown spiritually, I have become able to see others without my own interests at heart. Simply, I don't have to take everything personally, nor does everything have to be about me. Not always being self-conscious offers me tremendous relief.

I want to remember each day that when I think too much and do too much, I can lose my receptivity to the natural flow of life. When I move into the silent place of my heart and persist, I become aware of the small voice within guiding me gently on my path. I receive promptings and little flashes of inspiration and clarity as my mind becomes quieter and quieter.

I know only too well that it takes patience and time for the mind to quiet down. I love the quotation from the Persian mystic Rumi: "Don't be satisfied with poems and stories of how things have gone with others, unfold your own myth." For me, this means unfolding my own unique connection and relationship with God.

I have come to know there is a presence of something else,

very real, that is everywhere in our lives. This something, which I now call God, pervades all that is, including ourselves. For many years I failed to know it. I veered from it. I looked for it in relationships, in achievements—simply, outside of myself. Then I learned it was within me all the time. I truly thought marriage, health, material assets, being needed, being useful, or receiving recognition would bring me sustaining happiness. I didn't know I needed to return to my true self.

While I have much to learn, more and more I feel as if I belong now. I don't feel on the periphery of life. If I happen to see a golf tournament on the television or hear someone talking about it, I lean into the joy of the magnificent game. I have so much respect for what it takes to have a disciplined mind. Yes, I have heard about his new life and seen him on television. I smile. I am happy he is happy.

I have respect for the truth-tellers, the ones who lean into life and don't run for outside refuge when life throws a curveball. I believe one of the great disciplines is remembering what is essential in the midst of all the chaos of life. What has become more essential is the knowing that I belong, that I am enough, that I am not alone.

On my journey I was introduced to the work of Joseph Campbell. I was very drawn to his philosophies. One of his phrases is "Follow your bliss." The words that follow this phrase are not so well-known: "and if you do, unseen hands will open doors that you did not know existed."

The "unseen hands" and ones that I could see came again and again to me. I am grateful.

My prayer for you who have read my story is, whatever has happened in your life, whatever you may have believed in or dreamed of, please consider that it is in the past now. I believe we all are "stumbling toward the light." I also believe that when we stop and truly listen, there is a call in each of our hearts to return to who we really are. We have only to call with a sincere voice, and help will come.

It's late in the day. As the sun makes her way down, I know her light will be there tomorrow. My prayer is that, just as Barbara took Moe's hand and Moe took mine, each of us is open to taking someone's hand to help light the way.

I want my final words each day to always be, "Thank you. Simply, thank you."

Appendix of Blog Entries

❧ *The Humbling Power of Pain*

Maybe you can relate to this topic and maybe not. My intention is not to tell you what to do or make myself appear "right." Within my heart is a well of hope and desire to share my experience, and telling my truth is the only way I know how. I don't have all the answers, and I am not perfect, thank goodness.

I will admit that not too long ago, I wanted to have all the answers. I wanted to appear perfect to everyone. Experiencing pain is not a comfortable feeling. In fact, sometimes I want to run from it. I want to avoid going down into the depths of my being, afraid of what I might find. This was, of course, until I realized something miraculous about pain. It can make us realize that what we have inside is greater than we ever imagined. Pain truly has the power to heal when touched with a compassionate hand.

The day I was confronted with divorce, I was shocked. To this day I have never again experienced such a level of pain in my heart. I crumbled inside. I had never known a human being could feel so much discomfort from emotional discontent.

After three years, I have learned to enter the pain I used to bypass. Sometimes I dive right in, cry, weep, sleep, and awaken again stronger and more aware. I have practiced allowing myself to go into the pain. Just the other day, I was invited once again to enter that place I have come to know as my greatest teacher. As I write this, I feel a sense of courage and pride within myself in a humble way.

There were years when I wouldn't have considered pain a good thing. To make it go away, I would shop or people-please. When I look back, I see I missed out on many opportunities to learn from my suffering and move forward in love and kindness. Instead I stuffed my feelings so far down that it was inevitable, when they did come up, that they were going to create quite a blast.

This post was inspired by a recent shift in the way I experience pain, one that caught me by surprise *big time.* The other day I wrote a post on my thoughts about the color beige and how judgmental some people are about it. I was offended by a few comments, which naturally I took personally. Instead of sitting with the feeling and breathing, I raced in my mind and reacted. I didn't stop and ask myself the one question that has become my new best friend: "Is this going to make you feel good later?" The answer would have been no. I consciously made the choice to take offense, which I am sure we can all relate to.

I beat myself up for days about this and experienced a level of suffering I hadn't in a long time. I felt my feelings but took them to the extreme. I crushed myself into little pieces, telling myself I was not worthy or courageous. I was pathetic and should shut the entire blog down. Yes, I actually did this. Can you relate?

I meditated to quiet my mind, but the triggers came back. My mind crept back into old habits again. So I went to sleep. When I woke up, I took my dogs on a walk and tried to stay as present as possible. In those brief moments of clear presence, I noticed my pain had dissolved.

I later thought about all those times when I listened to people who were trying to get me out of my pain because they loved me. If it weren't for feeling the feelings of pain and of no ground under my feet, I wouldn't be able to share this with you today.

I have come to welcome pain from the past and the present.

It is what makes me relate to others and give them the empathy we all deserve. If I had no pain, if all that existed was pure joy 100 percent of the time, I would not be of help to anyone.

I am human. I believe my purpose is to serve others. My service happens to come in the form of my story, which will be released soon.

If you find yourself in pain, I invite you to enter it with a humble and soft heart and notice the lessons you learn from it. If we constantly run from the things that scare us, how will we ever learn? Won't those things keep coming back harder and harder until we have no ground to stand on? My mantra has become "Feel it. Experience it. Surrender to the flow of life."

I would like to point out one important aspect of my new realization about feeling pain and consciously choosing to enter the feelings that surface. I do not walk around crying or weeping while I am feeling pain. This is a big misconception. I have come to know that for me, I can experience any level of suffering and be a part of a conversation at the same time.

Pain has been a humbling experience. I no longer walk around feeling arrogant and better than anyone else just because I have come to know a *few* things about life (for me). I am like you, trying my best and hoping to learn a lot along the way.

Humbly yours,

Jocelyn

❧ *Allowing Someone to Be*

There are many persons who, out of the goodness of their hearts, want to see their neighbors flourish, not realizing what a dishonor they are doing by interfering in their neighbors' personal journeys and freedom to be who they are.

The last few weeks have been what I would call enlightening. But before they came to be "light," they were dark and heavy. Life is not always milk and honey, and for this I am grateful. It has been my practice over the last few years to recognize when I live in moments of duality: good/bad, right/wrong, or easy/hard. In my short time of practicing this principle, I have come to see where living and breathing in a world of duality has been my main source of sadness, pain, discomfort, and lack. It is not always easy to live without thinking in terms of duality, but I am getting there. One day at a time, my consciousness is shifting in a way I never knew possible.

When I slow down enough to realize the shift that has become a more natural part of my interior, I am in awe of how my mind has become less of the master. My mind had been on autopilot for years through cultural conditioning and religious beliefs. It is hard to believe I actually thought at one time that wearing white after Labor Day was "bad," and that if I lost a friend on Facebook, I wasn't worthy of being someone's friend. I was experiencing the world through my conditioned mind. It was in desperate need of some shampoo—the strong stuff that strips away all the buildup.

I like to call my new way of viewing the world "fruitage." When a tree is rooted deep in the earth, it has an opportunity to receive all the goodness from the minerals and Mother Nature's vitamins, right? Does an orange tree need to be told when to produce fruit? No. Does a lemon need to be connected to its source to ripen? Yes. My journey to this point has been to realize this fruitage and share it with the world in whatever way I am led. When I am connected, still, and aware, I can produce fruit. It can look like acceptance, love, lack of judgment, and, in my most recent experience, allowing others the freedom to be who they are, which is what led me to this post in the first place.

There is someone in my life whom I care deeply about. I want to see her succeed more than anything in the world. I began noticing a few things about this person that made me feel sad, and I immediately wanted to dive in and rescue her from her choices. To watch someone live in denial is one of the hardest things I have ever done. I watched myself become more involved in the story I was creating and actually started to plan some sort of intervention.

Then I paused and listened within for twenty-four hours. I needed forty-eight in the end, but what I came to was this: I am not here to rescue anyone, no matter how dire the situation is. (I do believe when children are directly involved, then action is necessary.) It is not my responsibility to show others what they are doing that could drastically change the course of their lives.

Does this sound like something we are taught to do? I don't know about you, but I was never taught to sit back and watch someone hit rock bottom. I have always been a helper, even when no one was asking for help, so this situation has been very difficult for me.

In my knowing, it is dangerous to step into someone else's world and tell her what she should and shouldn't be doing. I am not the person for that. Each person has a soul, and I am not it. When the desire to help was removed, a weight was lifted off me, and I felt a sense of inner peace I had not felt for those long two days. Like I said, she has a soul. She has a Comforter, Creator, God, whatever you want to call it, and I am not It. My belief that she will come to know her own answers was my version of helping her, as strange as it may sound.

It may seem harsh or even unkind to allow someone to fall or hit rock bottom, but at the end of the day, it is the only thing that will catapult her into knowing who she really is. My personal experience was just that. I had lied to myself for years, thinking I could stay in a relationship and sell my soul at the same time. I was eventually taken under the waves and hit rock bottom. Looking at every wound deeply and gaining the tools to heal them was my only way out of that style of living. It was only then I began to journey into a new vision for my life. I am glad no one saved me or tried to. It was necessary for me to endure such pain to know what healing truly felt like.

At the time, those around me allowed me the freedom to be who I was and walk each step of the way in my own shoes. They knew one day I would receive new ones. Today it is my sincere intention to help others find their own—*when they ask for help.*

I share this in hopes it may serve as a support for you or someone you may know. Please do not take this as direct advice for your situation. It is only my way of sharing my thoughts and experience. You have your own guide right within you. If you are quiet and listen, you will know exactly what to do.

Thank you for being here,

Jocelyn

Embracing Disappointment with Love and a Daily Practice

My head has been quite full these last two months with the question of purpose and living a meaningful life. I cannot help but constantly wonder if I am honoring my soul's purpose here or if my ego is leading me down a path of becoming "famous." It is a natural tendency for me to attempt to figure things out and analyze them to death. In the end, I always land in the same place—the silent and still point within myself where the answers are awakened.

In a contemplative, silent moment, I was led to the answer. I can only describe this feeling as a quiet, warm blanket over my inner life, wrapping itself around every fiber of my heart and soul. My mind was quiet and still for what seemed like eternity, and I heard with my inner ear the words "Go forward and just love." So this is what I will do. It begins with this blog. Today I will infuse love into the world by sharing my experience of how I learned to transform disappointment with love.

In my thirty-five years I have had my fair share of disappointing moments. While I have done a lot of intensive work in this area, I appreciate the significance disappointment has in my life. There were times when my mind would spin and spiral downward whenever disappointment sneaked in the side door.

I felt the desire to change, to obtain release from the negative feelings disappointment brought along. It seemed important to understand why I was feeling this emotion that would literally take over my entire day.

It became clear my expectations of others and of myself were simply out of alignment with reality. There were times when I couldn't get over that someone hadn't called me back after a week when I considered the topic we were discussing "important." My day would be filled with constant thoughts of disappointment, not to mention the big questions: "What is wrong with me? Why hasn't she called back?"

When it came to feeling disappointed in myself—well, that is where it got U-G-L-Y. Shaming myself and degrading my self-worth was rife in those days. By the time the sun went down, I was in a million pieces.

It has become my daily practice to pause, breathe, and align myself with the inner stillness we all carry within. In the beginning, I found it nearly impossible to unleash my mind and let it go. It had become my master and fought tooth and nail to stay that way.

After a period of months, it became natural to breathe consciously and take a moment to practice the principle of seeing disappointment as what *is* and not making it any more than that. The practice of seeing through appearances with the outer eye is something I strive to do every single minute, hour, and day in order to experience harmony in my inner and outer life. Ultimately, embracing the emotions that fill my mind makes me aware that there is more—more peace to be revealed, and that is a daily practice in itself.

It is amazing how one emotion can be the driving force in moving us forward, isn't it?

When I began translating negative emotions of any kind into love, I felt the shift, the freedom, and the ability to live by grace. The kind of love I am talking about is not a Valentine love. It is not lust either. The love I am speaking of comes from the soul, the place where inner peace flows out from within and soothes every moment with soft notes of harmony.

I realize this approach to emotions may seem unconventional to the outer world. I have come to know that when the faculties of the soul are on the field, there is nothing but inner peace to be experienced.

Wishing you and everyone in your day a beautiful string of moments,

Jocelyn

❦ *In the Pursuit of Presence*

*You are where you are supposed to be
because that is where you are.*

—Buddha

When I look down at my feet, I am reminded that I am right where I am. If I close my eyes and take a deep breath, I am led into the innermost being of my life, which is more telling than the outer, I can assure you.

There was a time when I was terribly afraid of taking a deeper look into my inner life. I was in fear of what I might find or, even scarier, learn about myself. It didn't matter who told me. It could have been Buddha himself. I wasn't going to push through one more bit. I was stubborn and scared until the day I was given news that shocked me so much, I thought my life was over. Today, I can say with my whole heart that this news saved my life. Hearing a divorce was imminent was a saving grace. It ultimately gave me my self back, but not before a lot of searching and listening.

I would like to return to this part of the quote: "where you are." Many women ask me how I could accept where I was at a time of so much pain. The truth is, I had no choice. When I was told my marriage was over, I couldn't speak. Literally. I was sitting across from my then-husband, and my lip was quivering, but I did not want him to see me fall apart. Yes, that is how good I was at hiding my feelings (when I actually felt them). When I got up from our discussion, I remember walking into the bathroom and crying so hard my false eyelashes fell out. I was already feeling lonely and abandoned, but there was something inside of me that whispered, "Keep going ... You can do this."

I wasn't a stranger to difficult tasks or hard emotions, but I was a stranger to being emotionally sober when it came to pain. After all, I was right where I was because that was where I was meant to be. I remember telling my coach at the time that I needed proof everything would be *okay.* You see, she herself had already experienced similar situations, and she had done the work to overcome and learn from them. But I hadn't—yet. I wanted to desperately though; I did. One day, I did.

My days and nights were spent learning to feel, accept, dive deep, and trust myself again. Essentially, I was returning to my self, a woman I barely knew. Being content with reality got easier. I think it was down to a few things I would like to share in case you ever find yourself or a friend in a similar situation. Please remember my intention is not to tell others what they should be doing. Writing this is simply my way of extending my experience in hopes it may inspire others to take the next step

Do the Next Single Thing. The mind can be very strong and can often feel like a tornado. My mind was swirling all the time; I felt as though I were in a washing machine. Moreover, I could never get out until I began the practice of repeating my mantra: "Just do the next single thing that will add peace to this moment."

Sometimes it would be to drink some water. Other times it would be to stand up and walk to the door. In my knowing, the mind can master a situation whereas the heart gently allows the situation to flow naturally and softly. The mind doesn't feel; the heart and soul do. When we can learn to quiet the mind a tad, we can give our hearts permission to lead us to peace and love. Keep in mind this is not to divert someone into escaping feelings;

it mainly acts as a support when the mind wants to go on a roller coaster ride.

Read Uplifting Material. Reading material that will move us forward is essential in dealing with any situation in life. I realized keeping my consciousness filled with truth was important. Take a moment to look through your library and choose a book that will fill your heart with hope and inspiration. Today, I do not read fiction books, only the material directly related to my spiritual practice. Keep it light; keep it meaningful!

Be Mindful and Selective. Talking to everyone about "where you are" can be healing as well as harmful. I remember sharing my experience with someone once, only to receive a handful of advice that made me feel worse. Be mindful and choose people you know will support where you are in your life, not try and "fix" you. I also learned to be up front with friends and make them aware that I wanted to be heard, not advised, which worked quite well.

Design Matters. With every good design, there is a product that functions seamlessly. I began to design my day with a plan that allowed for flexibility but also kept me on track. Providing too much open time and no organization gave me too much time to think about the past or future.

Be Gentle with Yourself. I must have heard this one million times through my recovery: "Be gentle with yourself." It's fairly simple. Be your own best friend and gently remind yourself every day that you are doing the very best you can.

Trust the Process. We can revert to the quotation I gave you at the beginning. We are where we are because that is exactly where we are supposed to be. This is a helpful reminder when hope is fading and thoughts of "why me?" start rolling in. I have come to know the lessons are in the process. In order to move forward, we must fully embrace every aspect. I found trusting the process very hard until I did it enough times to witness the reward acceptance brings.

After three intense years of returning to my essential self, I have used every one of the practices shared here. I invite you to integrate these into your own day and watch the miracles happen. If you know of a friend dealing with a challenging time, please do share!

While I do not intend to perfect them in any way, each of these practices has led me to that still point within that tells me all is well, no matter what my mind says.

✍ Before Dawn—
The Beauty of Silence

If anyone had told me three years ago I would be swapping my iPhone for time in silence before dawn, I might have told them they were out of touch with reality, big time. My journey has been a beautiful sequence of smiles and tears, and along the way I have learned to embrace the challenging times, knowing they too shall pass. Silence is not a stranger to me, and in all honesty for a long time it is where I spent most of my day. The difference between then and now is that the quiet periods are centered in my heart and not my mind.

In my experience, silence is the only way I know to receive answers to the questions my soul gently poses. Every morning before the sun comes up, I spend at least ten minutes in complete silence and stillness, opening the inner ear and listening for guidance. Does this sound scary to you? Well, it should. Not all of us are taught to quiet the mind and still our center. Silence is scary when the mind is the master.

The only way to slow down the mind (for me) is to let it go and ramble on, knowing it will quiet and lose its power to stillness. The mind loses power when the soul begins to reign supreme. When I first sat in silence, I felt like my head was a yo-yo going up and down, quickly. I wasn't sitting in the lotus position and my hands were not doing anything funny. I was allowing myself to be still and hoping my mind would follow.

One day it finally did. It was like a homecoming of sorts. I knew I was able to sit in silence and receive something beyond *this world.* As I write this, tears are forming in my eyes. I remember the days I longed to hear my soul and to know there was something beyond what I could hear, smell, taste, and touch.

As I became more comfortable with the lack of noise, it occurred to me I was deepening my level of awareness when it came to my inner life. This was where the real journey began. In the silence is soul guidance, and nothing is deeper than the soul as far as I know.

Do you spend moments in your day in complete silence? Have you found it to be helpful? Lately, I have spoken with some wonderful people who are excited to practice sitting in silence before dawn. If you would like to join me, please do!

Each day, set the intention to wake up and silence your mind. If you can only do it for a minute, that's fine. Each day you can extend it a little further until you don't even know how long you've been quiet.

In the silence, allow the mind to do what it wants. It will settle as you focus on your breathing. Listen with your inner ear. Open yourself to hear your soul speak to you. I know you will hear something profound—it is inevitable.

This practice requires mindfulness and a deep sense of desire to enter silence. If you want it badly enough, you will be like me and forget the phone, e-mails, IG comments, Facebook likes, and all that. In exchange, you will hear the pulse of your soul, which is what creates heaven on earth for us and everyone in our day.

I would like to thank Moe Ross, my mentor, for leading me to the door of silence and communing within to receive my own answers that propel me on my path.

❧ *Ambition to Meaning*

Being ambitious was always a part of my daily structure. From a young age I, like so many of you, was taught to be a go-getter and to do something with life. I thought that meant I needed to go to college and get a four-year degree—maybe even stay a little longer and get my master's degree. I felt like a failure because I had neither. This made me ambitious and hypersensitive to perfection in other areas of my life, which ultimately led me to my knees. The deeper story here is the way my life evolved from one of ambition to one of meaning.

Ambition was what drove me for many years. I took workshops to expand my knowledge base and appear smarter to those I spoke with. I moved halfway across the country to become certified in equine therapy. I began multiple businesses, throwing myself into each one as if it were the "answer."

What I found was a sense of emptiness with each blog, Web site, workshop, and conference. I worked hard day and night for something I didn't truly want. But I had been brought up to finish what I started, so I did. Talk about torture! I wrote less and less and allowed my creative mind to take over a little bit more, which led to days when I would walk around and relearn how to be still with myself.

Over time I realized my ambition occupied the driver's seat in my heart and soul. I decided that had to change. Nevertheless, I learned a lot from all my adventures. I am grateful for all of the skills I can now pass on to others who are in need. The path I have been on for the last three years has been one of immense self-discovery, and one I am happy to share with others.

With each blog, the content has traveled deeper and deeper into my inner life. What has happened for me is somewhat difficult to put into words, but I will do my best to explain it in a simple way. I crave meaning in my life. Ambition has dissolved because I realize that I, of my own self, can do nothing. Whenever the "I" is involved, there is a sense of getting instead of *giving*. Simply, I feel better when I give. The days of doing things *just* for the fun of it are over.

I realize this may sound harsh. Taking conversations to a higher level is one example of living a life of meaning. Being of service to others is another. The most profound lesson for me so far is allowing myself to be led to the lessons I need to learn to grow and expand my heart to love more.

When I started my inner journey, I longed for meaning in my life. The shoes, handbags, butlers, drivers, and private planes were not doing it for me anymore. I wanted more substance in my life, and I asked for it. What I didn't know was the journey I would take over the course of nearly four years and how much I would learn about what living a meaningful life means to me.

At the end of the day, living a life of meaning begins with kindness. I am learning my new definition of that word every single day.

❧ My Life's Sincere Contribution

When I was a little girl, I would ride around on my pony with wind flowing through my hair and dirt on my face. I longed to understand how I was going to succeed in this so-called life I was centered in. The school I attended was a magnet school, so our curriculum was slightly different from that of other schools. We were constantly encouraged to swim in the sea of creativity.

During a pep rally one afternoon, the entire school gathered in the cafeteria for a motivational talk. By the end, we were all shouting "S-U-C-C-E-S-S!" The only thing I was certain of at that point was that I would never spell *success* wrong, ever. Now, twenty-five years later, I am beginning to understand the meaning of success for me. It can be summed up in one very simple yet profound word—*consciousness*.

As I look at my life today, I am grateful for everything that has taken place and the lessons that have led me to my version of success, even though the journey is far from complete. I can't help but think being successful is an ongoing process that continuously jumps from one infinite hopscotch box to the next. I see success as contributing to life and making it a better place.

How does that happen exactly? For me, it stems from consciousness. Developing my consciousness is something I never thought I would do, mainly because I didn't know what it meant. It took a core-shaking divorce to bring me to my knees and open my interior life to a new design. My mentor, Moe Ross, led me to the door of consciousness, and I have never looked back. I found myself required to take the steps necessary to evolve into a higher version of the little girl on the horse who so longed to know who she was and what her purpose was on earth. That is exactly what I have done ever since.

I have come to know success isn't about awards, recognition, or ribbons. The number of followers or friends I have on social media does not matter to me one single bit. For me, success is contributing to the world in the highest sense of *being*, not *doing*, from my center. *Being* allows me to be led from my heart, as opposed to *doing*, which for me is always from my concept-filled mind.

I have also come to realize this is not as easy as flipping a switch to on from off. The journey of discovering what success feels like is downright hard. It is my practice every day to ensure I do not slip back into old patterns that block my consciousness from rising.

Success to me looks a little like this:

- As I wake up every morning, I consciously remember that "I" am not in control of my day. There is a source beyond my understanding, and I am divinely guided in every situation.
- Reading a negative response or e-mail does not disturb me. I can move on naturally without repeating a mantra or sitting quietly for some time to let the feeling go.
- I share my story of experience and hope with other women to support them when they might not have anyone or anything to hold on to.
- I see through appearances, looking deeper inside others and knowing they are not what they appear to be when my mind sees them as "mean."

- I know nothing is the answer. Clothes, candles, makeup, or fans are not the answer. The only answer is consciousness and how I will use that to fulfill my calling.
- I allow life to flow rather than making it go in the direction I want it to. Letting go of the life I envisioned for the life I was meant to live ever since I was born is a jump worth taking.

Obviously there are many more, and as much as I would like to share them with you, I keep some of them sacred until the seed is in full bloom. Consciousness is a constant state of evolution, and I know I have a long way to go.

For today, I can say I have felt success through a project I am working on with my mentor, and I cannot wait to share it with you when the time is right.

So the girl who once lived to feel the wind in her hair and a sense of divine purpose is holding steady to success as consciousness, rising.

This post is not intended to teach you anything. It is simply a sharing of my experience in the hope it may inspire you to join me on the journey if you have ever felt the desire to walk a different way.

Jocelyn

❧ *Criticism*

Growing up, I was taught never to criticize others verbally for their beliefs, no matter how far those beliefs differed from mine. My parents taught me to stand firm in my own beliefs and not to allow others to sway me. During those years of galloping my pony across an open field, it never occurred to me someone could criticize me for what I did, thought, or believed. It wasn't in my consciousness—period.

Throughout my high school and college years, when I read more newspapers and celebrity magazines, I participated in judging others for their choices in clothing or their actions, not consciously understanding what I was doing. During my journey of discovering myself, I went through many periods of criticizing myself for not being able to meditate or sit in stillness. My lower self beat the real me up so badly I was often left in a puddle of tears on the floor.

Even today I have times when I criticize myself, but it begins and ends with the thought. There is no action attached to the belief my mind has created. I see now that I criticize and judge myself less because I do not criticize and judge others. What other people believe or think is none of my business.

However, recently being severely criticized for my behavior left me humbled, raw, and open to a new way of viewing the experience I had lived.

There I was, sitting in a chair, thinking I was going to discuss my life with someone who had asked about it. (I will leave names out of the story to respect those involved.) A person sat down next to me and asked me when I was ever going to change. This person said I had hurt everyone in the room for the last three years due to my time away while dealing with a divorce and building a new life.

Keep in mind that I had never before been so much as pulled aside for being rude or mean to anyone. This was a brand-new experience for me. For two hours I took a verbal lashing, said nothing or very little, and allowed the others to share their experiences of me.

I realized in one moment early on that I was not responsible for the experiences of other people. I am simply concerned with witnessing my own behavior. Timm (my partner) looked at me in shock, as if I might get up and walk out. I gave him a look of "It's all right—let's allow this to run its course."

After all the people spoke, I was left feeling a little bruised. But mainly I felt a deep sense of acceptance and absolutely no desire to defend myself. After all, why would I ever attempt to change people's experience of me if they were so certain I was a particular way? I cannot do anything about the way someone feels about me. I know enough to understand it is mostly a projection of their own interior.

When I got home, I burst into tears. I had to release the energy that I had taken on in that room. I know some people who have a very high consciousness can take heat like that. But had I not been aligned with myself that day, the outcome might have been very different. I was glad I was able to cry tears of release instead of pain.

You may be thinking this is an odd thing to share, and what in the world does it have to do with living mindfully? Well, I am sharing this because it is simply my way of giving back. If my experience can help someone see a similar situation differently and rise above the mind, which believes in good and bad, then I have fulfilled a purpose today. If I hadn't instilled the practice of mindfulness every day, I would have walked out of that meeting or said a few things I would have regretted. I didn't. I sat tall and noble and listened deeply to what others thought of me. I was in a state of acceptance. I knew that the people in front of me were not mean, rude, or critical. They were human, and I am well aware that I teach others how to treat me.

So what now? Well, I don't engage as much with those people. However, I still love them deeply. I don't find myself moving toward those who cannot accept me for who I am. If I saw them on the street, I would hug them and help them if they asked, but I would not participate in allowing the same sort of experience to happen again.

This is all part of the alignment I talked about in the last blog post. If a person or group is not aligned with my inner compass, then I simply don't lean toward them. Acceptance is a beautiful thing. Where there is no judgment, there is inner peace. If only it were so easy! But we can practice and keep moving forward until this state of acceptance becomes natural and flows like water within our being.

I hope you have found this helpful if you have ever experienced being criticized for something you have said or done. If you know someone who may be going through a similar situation, I encourage you to share this post with him or her as a supportive tool.

From my heart,
Jocelyn

When Friendships Drift yet Never Part Within

Friendships have always been a sticky subject for me. I think I am beginning to understand why as I travel deeper to find the answers from my teacher hidden within. This week has been wonderful week and at the same time a very revealing week. At one time, I was the kind of girl who wanted everyone to like her. Today I am the kind of woman who doesn't need everyone to like her. My biggest teacher? Friendships that drift apart. The lesson? Learn to let go of what you cannot control and love anyway.

Even though I feel sometimes I have a handle on my desire to be liked, it still has a tendency to creep in and sneak around my heart and mind like a vine wrapping itself around a light post.

Occasionally my mind will attempt to show me what is wrong with me. It takes me to the cleaners and back. Then sometimes my mind is slow enough to realize I am not here to take inventory of other people's behavior. I am only here to witness my own and act according to who I have decided to be. I am human, and this is not always easy.

My heart has been heavy at times and full of pain, but I always get through it—always.

This week I finally came to terms with a friendship that drifted away almost a year ago. The truth is, after six years of spending many hours laughing, traveling, celebrating, crying, and planning with my friend, she is now gone and has a new best friend. We didn't have the period where we drifted from one another slowly. We flat-out had our cords cut and that was it.

When it happened, I was shocked. I didn't know any way to handle it other than to take responsibility for my own behavior. I wasn't about to change my principles to keep a friend, even if she was my *best* friend.

There is a quote from a spiritual teacher that goes something like this: "People change and forget to tell the other person." Well, that was us. I had changed, and she wasn't so sure she liked all the transformation. I had stopped being so agreeable and the "yes" woman, and this is of course hard for some people to accept.

The day our friendship ended, I felt relief. I didn't have to try to be someone else for somebody to like me. But as I took that deep sigh of relief, I felt incredibly sad, and I guess I have been for the last eleven months.

In my recent years of practicing not to escape pain, I have recognized the level of pain that leads to deep insight for myself. As I write this, I can say I learned a lot from my friend. To me, she will always be my best friend. No matter what, she will always have residence in my heart. Physical separation might be what is apparent now, but I send her love every time I think of her. To be honest, that's all we both need. Judging, condemning, and comparing do no good and certainly don't move me forward. My mind doesn't always want to take this gentle route, but I make it do so until it surrenders to a force way bigger than it is—*my heart*.

I felt led to share this with you all in case you find yourself in a similar situation with a friend. Please note this is not an attempt to teach or preach. This is simply to share my experience in the hope that you may never feel alone if you are experiencing a friendship that has drifted.

I am not even going to tell you to remember something special because I don't know what you should remember. You have your own teacher within. It is there I have found a peace beyond my understanding.

CPSIA information can be obtained
at www.ICGtesting.com
Printed in the USA
FSOW01n1044190116
15799FS

9 781480 824232